THE COMMISSIONER

A GUIDE TO SURVIVING AND THRIVING
ON COMMISSION INCOME

Peter Dunn

Cengage Learning PTR

CENGAGE
Learning·

Professional • Technical • Reference

Australia, Brazil, Japan, Korea, Mexico, Singapore, Spain, United Kingdom, United States

Professional • Technical • Reference

The Commissioner: A Guide to Surviving and Thriving on Commission Income
Peter Dunn

Publisher and General Manager, Cengage Learning PTR:
Stacy L. Hiquet

Associate Director of Marketing:
Sarah Panella

Manager of Editorial Services:
Heather Talbot

Senior Product Manager:
Mitzi Koontz

Project Editor/ Copy Editor:
Cathleen D. Small

Interior Layout Tech:
Bill Hartman

Indexer:
Sharon Shock

Proofreader:
Gene Redding

© 2015 Peter Dunn.

WCN: 01-100

CENGAGE and CENGAGE LEARNING are registered trademarks of Cengage Learning, Inc., within the United States and certain other jurisdictions.

For product information and technology assistance, contact us at
Cengage Learning Customer & Sales Support, 1-800-354-9706
For permission to use material from this text or product, submit all requests online at **cengage.com/permissions**
Further permissions questions can be emailed to
permissionrequest@cengage.com

All trademarks are the property of their respective owners.

All images © Peter Dunn unless otherwise noted.

Library of Congress Control Number: 2014953141

ISBN-13: 978-1-305-50492-9

ISBN-10: 1-305-50492-5

Cengage Learning PTR
20 Channel Center Street
Boston, MA 02210
USA

Cengage Learning is a leading provider of customized learning solutions with office locations around the globe, including Singapore, the United Kingdom, Australia, Mexico, Brazil, and Japan. Locate your local office at: **international.cengage.com/region**

Cengage Learning products are represented in Canada by Nelson Education, Ltd.

For your lifelong learning solutions, visit **cengageptr.com**

Visit our corporate website at **cengage.com**

Printed in the United States of America
1 2 3 4 5 6 7 16 15 14

To salespeople.
Salespeople eat what they kill.
May they never go hungry.

ACKNOWLEDGMENTS

This book wouldn't have been possible without the support and inspiration of a great number of people. From loved ones to colleagues, *The Commissioner* is the result of a team effort.

For me, it begins with my office staff. Beth Weingart has been my right hand for 10 years. Her dedication to our mission of bringing financial wellness to everyday people is remarkable. Thanks to Jasmin Snyder, who helped organize the curriculum out of my jumbled thoughts, and Alex Eaton for his research in the early going.

I'm certainly thankful for my longtime friend and business consultant CJ McClanahan. He helped me form the vision for this book, and his counsel has proven to be invaluable.

Without the team at Cengage Learning PTR, this book wouldn't see the light of day. Mitzi Koontz and Cathleen Small helped pull off the impossible under some pretty tough deadlines. Thanks to my longtime designer Lindsay Hadley, whose beautiful images help convey feeling on the cover of my books.

A vast number of people have inspired this effort in one way or another. That list includes but is not limited to: Marc Williams, Scott McKain, Neal Brown, Charlie Morgan, Mike D., Jim Kean, Dan Veto, and David Klain. The discussions with these individuals and their other forms of inspiration are often the fuel to my creative fire.

And finally, thanks to my wife Sarah, who helps provide a stable environment that allows me to write, create, and speak. Her sacrifices are as innumerable as they are loving.

ABOUT THE AUTHOR

Peter Dunn is an author, radio host, and personal finance expert who has developed content and curriculum for some of the world's largest financial companies. He was a financial advisor for nearly 15 years and managed several millions of dollars in assets. He is known for his down-to-earth and humorous approach that resonates with both consumers and financial industry insiders. He appears regularly on Fox News, Fox Business, and CNN Headline News, as well as several nationally syndicated radio programs. In 2012, Cision named him the fourth most influential personal finance broadcaster in the nation. Today, Peter's financial wellness firm develops financial wellness curricula for Fortune 500 companies.

Learn more at PeteThePlanner.com.

CONTENTS

Chapter 8: Making It Stick   141

Index   153

INTRODUCTION

You are the Commissioner. You are in charge of everything in your financial life. You make the final decisions. When you accepted your commission-based or variable compensation plan, you took the first step in taking control of your financial life. It's now time to take the second step.

I'm a Commissioner, too. We're a pretty big group. We are business owners, freelancers, realtors, pharmaceutical reps, call-center workers, car salespeople, financial planners, insurance agents, artists, waiters and waitresses, writers, and anyone else whose income fluctuates from month to month.

For nearly 15 years, I was compensated on a 100 percent commission basis. I remember sitting across the table from one particular customer a few years ago, calculating my potential commission in my head. I'm not proud of this now, and I certainly wasn't proud of it then. But my paychecks had been up and down, and if this deal had worked out, I might actually have found some stability. Unfortunately, math can be distracting, and the sales conversation started falling apart. I felt like Lenny from *Of Mice and Men*. The sale was my puppy. I petted the puppy too hard. The puppy died. No sale.

Financial stress and instability can create some serious professional challenges.

Variable income is all I've ever known. My first commission-income job was presented to me as a $150,000 opportunity. Aren't they all? I was 22 and interviewed for a job at a very large financial planning firm. The recruiter told me the average planner in the firm made $150,000, and there was no reason why I shouldn't achieve that level within the first year. Despite being one of the top two "new guys" that year, I didn't even come close to $150,000 in my first year. This is when I started to truly understand variable income. I (unrealistically) planned on making $150,000, I watched various amounts of money trickle in month after month, and at the end of the year I had nowhere near $150,000.

Not only did I not have $150,000, but I didn't even really know what I had. Each individual sale and commission check caused me to react. I was playing defense, and my fluctuating paycheck was on offense. Every paycheck had a new number. Every new number was an adventure. Would it be enough to pay my bills? Would it be enough to buy something awesome? No matter how I reacted and used the money, there was another new adventure coming the next week. I had to stop thinking of my income as a sale-to-sale, paycheck-to-paycheck adventure. I needed to start thinking of my income on a bigger scale. But my check was training me otherwise. How could I possibly create a reasonable financial life when my check was yo-yoing from great to tragic?

There was another problem. I kept selling myself phony ideas about my financial health. The hard truth about salespeople is they often sell themselves loads of misinformation in regard to their own financial life. Money earned is conveniently confused with money kept. Limitless income potential is commonly confused with financial stability. And control of income is often confused with financial self-control. I had all of these problems. Because once I proved to myself that I could generate sales and income, I became convinced I could create spending money on demand.

I constructed my financial life wrong. That's easy to do when you have no base income. When a salesperson is 100 percent commission, it's very difficult to create the simplest of financial tools, a budget. Variable income + overconfidence in your ability to create income on demand + no budget = a financial disaster.

How could this be? Salespeople are the doers. Salespeople are the revenue producers.

Salespeople aren't the accountants. Salespeople aren't the controller. And salespeople aren't the CFOs.

In many respects, this book is about keeping you in the business. At some point, the stresses of playing the yo-yo game are too much to deal with.

This book is for both commission-income earners and anyone with a variable income. Throughout the book, I will reference commission income quite frequently. If you aren't a commission-income earner, yet you have a variable income, then please know that I'm still referencing you and your income in the text. It just didn't make sense to consistently write "commission or variable income."

In many respects, it seems as though we are dealing with a chicken-or-the-egg scenario. Which comes first: professional success or financial stability? For years, I thought the answer was professional success. I believed the answer to almost any financial problem was more money. I no longer believe this. It's absurd to think that professional success alone can fix your finances. Professional success may bring resources, but it doesn't bring resourcefulness. That's a problem. The key to my financial stability, your financial stability, or anyone else's financial stability is resourcefulness. Who cares how many resources you earn, if you've proven yourself to be unresourceful?

The Commissioner will teach you exactly how to improve your resourcefulness. In addition, you will learn strategies for smoothing out the hard months and settling down during the amazing months. Your personal finances are going to enhance your ability to have a great career. It's time to put you back in charge of your financial life. You are the Commissioner.

CHAPTER 1

THE FLOW

What would happen if you were paid your entire annual income on January 1st? The mere thought of this is both exciting and terrifying. If you've struggled with budgeting in the past and you haven't addressed this problem, then getting paid your entire year's income on January 1st would be a disaster. Adding resources has never been a permanent solution to a lack of resourcefulness.

What if you received a paycheck at the end of each workday? Would that create budget challenges for you? If your annual income was $75,000 and you worked 250 days in a year, then you would receive a $300 paycheck every day you worked. Does this excite you? Scare you?

Or imagine being paid your future career earnings on the first day of your first real job. "Here's $2.5 million. Good luck!"

Your frequency of pay is arbitrary. Just because your company pays you once per week, twice per month, every other week, once per month, or once every decade, that doesn't mean you have to let it affect your financial life. In fact, NFL players get paid 17 weeks per year—that is, the 17 weeks of the regular season. And if they don't make the playoffs, NFL players don't see another regular paycheck for 35 weeks. Many people scoff at this because of the amount of money professional athletes get paid, but many people would struggle with this pay schedule in spite of what the pay scale might be.

The challenge comes from the fact that many of our financial obligations are billed on a monthly basis. Your mortgage/rent payment, car payment, and utilities require that you say hello every 30 days or so. But this mere inconvenience shouldn't dramatically impact your financial life. This is of no consequence for people who make a steady, consistent income. Sure, some people still struggle to create and maintain a budget, but it's not because of a variable income.

If managed improperly—as it often is—a commission or variable income can make regular monthly bills seem extraordinarily difficult. If you have a variable income, then you need to learn how to efficiently play your income against your expenses. You have to learn how to stop taking your cash flow for granted.

You wouldn't be alone if you selected your expenses before your income was determined. We make assumptions about income potential, sign documents, and before we know it, our mortgage payment accounts for 42 percent of our average monthly income. (By the way, that's bad.)

The most difficult aspect of intertwining fixed expenses and variable income is actually a byproduct of temporary success. We'll discuss various definitions of success throughout *The Commissioner*, but in this case we're talking about making major expense decisions and commitments during periods of sales success. Committing your future uncertain income to expenses that were inspired by sales success puts a tremendous amount of pressure on you, and frankly, many times the math just doesn't work. For example, if you have a brilliant quarter and then you set your spending based on your three-month income, you can create a quagmire of shortages if seasonality or normalcy returns to your situation.

The relationship between variable income and fixed expenses can create two major issues: math problems and financial stress. Whereas math problems are concrete and palpable, financial stress is a silent killer. One of the primary reasons why *The Commissioner* exists is to help you manage the financial stress that comes with a variable-income gig. Denying the existence and/or impact of financial stress is dangerous to your financial life and your career. But ignoring the buildup of financial stress in your life can be fatal. Not to be an alarmist, but financial stress, which seems like a mind issue, can quickly manifest itself into a physical health issue.

FINANCIAL STRESS

An AP-AOL poll, taken just before the economic meltdown of 2008, found that 27 percent of people who suffered from high levels of financial stress experienced ulcers or digestive-tract problems.[1] Only 8 percent of low-stress individuals suffered the same maladies. And 29 percent of the high-stress group dealt with severe anxiety, while only 4 percent of the low-stress group battled severe anxiety.

A September 2009 report in the *Chicago Tribune* noted that school counselors and psychologists found academic-performance issues from children whose parents were dealing with high levels of financial stress.[2] The parents' stress and anxiety trickled down to the children.

Financial stress has been linked not only to health issues, but also to loss of productivity, presenteeism, and poor on-the-job financial decision-making. A 2014 PricewaterhouseCoopers

---

[1] AP-AOL poll, conducted March 24–April 3, 2008. See surveys.ap.org for full results.

[2] Leslie Brody, "Recession's Toll on Children: Parents Aren't the Only Ones Who Suffer when Jobs Are Lost and Money Is Tight," *Chicago Tribune*, Sept. 20, 2009.

financial wellness survey found that 24 percent of people with financial stress experienced loss of productivity.[3] Presenteeism issues were also unveiled in this survey. Presenteeism is the concept of being at work physically but not mentally. And 39 percent of respondents admitted to spending at least three hours per week thinking about or dealing with their financial problems while at work.

At first glance, these statistics appear to be your employer's problem, not yours. But that assertion couldn't be any further from the truth. If you are experiencing financial stress, your financial stress is your problem. You are the assailant, the victim, the cop, the jury, the warden, and the solution. Get your head around that. You aren't only the problem, but also the solution.

If you're a commission-income earner, earning more money isn't the solution. Taking control of your inflows and outflows is a solution. Normalizing your income is a solution. Financial stress doesn't go away when you have a big quarter. Believe it or not, your unwillingness to look at the math is a huge part of the problem.

---

[3] www.pwc.com/en_US/us/private-company-services/ publications/assets/pwc-employee-financial-wellness-survey-2014-results.pdf.

MATH PROBLEMS

How much money did you make last quarter? Go ahead: Put down this book, grab your paystubs, and do the math. As you know, especially if you are in sales, there are 13 weeks in a quarter. What was your weekly income, if you were to divide your entire quarterly income by 13? For instance, if your net pay was $17,500 last quarter, then your weekly income over that same timeframe averaged $1,346. But based on how the world works and how business develops, it's unlikely that your actual weekly paycheck was in a tight standard deviation of $1,346. Standard deviation? It's learning time.

Prepare yourself—things are about to get technical.

Standard deviation is a measure of how much variance from the average exists. In other words, if your average weekly income is $1,346, then standard deviation measures how far typical paychecks tend to be from the average paycheck. Life and budgeting are easy when you hit $1,346 per week. But what if you were paid $786 in a particular week? This question is one of the primary reasons for this book. What do you do when you are averaging a certain pay level, but some paychecks are below that level? And how does this affect the bills that are due on a regular monthly schedule?

The lower the standard deviation for a set of weekly or monthly income numbers, the easier it is to budget. The higher the standard deviation for a set of weekly or monthly income numbers, the more difficult it is to budget.

Consider these three different sets of weekly income numbers. Take a look at the standard deviation and mean (average) of each set.

Set 1

Week 1:	$1,200
Week 2:	$900
Week 3:	$1,500
Week 4:	$1,800
Mean (average):	$1,350
Standard Deviation:	387.29833

Set 2

Week 1:	$1,350
Week 2:	$1,450
Week 3:	$1,250
Week 4:	$1,350
Mean (average):	$1,350
Standard Deviation:	81.64966

Set 3

Week 1:	$2,100
Week 2:	$600
Week 3:	$1,650
Week 4:	$1,050
Mean (average):	$1,350
Standard Deviation:	659.5453

Which income scenario is the easiest to work with? Which is the most difficult? Set 2 is the easiest to work with due to the low standard deviation. And Set 3 is the most challenging, despite the extraordinarily large first week's income. Don't get distracted by the frequency of pay in this example. The sets could just as easily have been monthly, and the same problems would persist.

You can calculate your income's standard deviation at PeteThePlanner.com/commissioner-tools.

And this is where commission and variable income get excruciatingly tricky: Even higher than average paychecks can create budgeting issues. The perceived standard solution for people dealing with budgeting and financial-stress issues is to simply make more money. By earning more than your average pay in a given paycheck, you hope to curb the math and stress issues that plague your life. But sadly, a lack of money isn't the problem.

I've personally witnessed highly compensated individuals struggling for years because they couldn't deal with the timing of their income versus the timing of their bills. These people weren't lazy; they just never took the time to fix the problem. But more realistically, they didn't know what the problem was—and unfortunately, what the problem still is. Do you know what the only advantage salaried individuals have over commission and variable income-earners is? People with salaries have structured, regimented pay. This makes financial decision-making easier, budgeting easier, and debt management easier.

Keep pulling back on the shot for a moment. Let's say you make $350,000 over a four-year period. Does this in any way impact your ability to progress financially? Nope. It's a trick. Four years is as arbitrary a timeframe as one year is. The only thing that truly impacts our lives is the frequency of our bills.

The arbitrary nature of your income becomes a negative if you don't do anything about it, especially if you have a variable or commission-based income. So if the frequency of your income is arbitrary, how can you leverage this for good?

How much money do you pay your mortgage company every year? If you pay them $1,500/month, then you pay them $18,000 per year. How much do you pay your mortgage company every day? You pay them $49.32. But it's ridiculous to think of funding your mortgage obligation this way. It's just as ridiculous as your variable income is. Now it's time to match up two very arbitrarily timed numbers: your income and your expenses.

FORCING YOUR INCOME TO MATCH YOUR EXPENSES

One of the natural reactions to a variable income is to make your expenses unnecessarily variable, too. "If I have a bad month, I can always dine out less," you've undoubtedly thought. And "if I have a good month, then life gets good again" is probably your other common refrain. The problem with this methodology is that you will never get ahead. You will always ask yourself whether you had a good month prior to making a buying decision. And while asking yourself this somewhat reasonable question seems prudent, it certainly isn't any way to live.

Yo-yoing your expenditures based on your income is incredibly stressful. If you make every financial decision based on your last pay period, you will start to measure your self-worth based on your last pay period. Don't do that. The old adage "you're only as good as your last performance" isn't true. And if you adopt this false mentality, your financial stress can become debilitating.

FINANCIAL STRESS

One of the most important aspects of *The Commissioner* is learning to manage financial stress. Mismanagement of financial stress can bring down even the greatest salesperson. You may not even realize that financial stress is present in your life, often due to denial. For some, admitting the presence of financial stress seems akin to admitting weakness. I find this very common misconception to be absurd. Identifying stress is the first step in alleviating stress. Burying your head in the sand, especially in relation to financial stress, is a horrible, ineffective strategy.

As uncomfortable as it might be, thoroughly consider each of the questions below. Be honest with yourself.

1. What do you believe your current financial stress level to be? (1 is low stress and 10 is high stress.)

2. Has your income in the last three months been higher, lower, or the same as in previous months?

3. If your income dipped by $2,000 next month, would you take the money out of savings, borrow money, or not be affected at all?

4. How well did you do with the money from your last "thriving" (exceptionally good) month? (1 is you were moneywise, and 10 is you blew it.)

5. Do you have a positive or a negative net worth? (You will learn to calculate this on page 104.)

6. If your income has increased in the last 12 months, has your debt decreased and your savings increased?

7. Are you contributing to your company-sponsored retirement plan (or any retirement plan, including an IRA) up to the employer match?

8. Do you tend to make poorer financial decisions on payday?

9. Do you openly discuss your financial situation with your significant other?

10. Does spending money make you feel better about your financial situation?

I'm sure you're looking for some sort of answer key to the above stress test. But you already know what the *right* answers are. The key is whether or not your honest assessment of yourself matches the right answers. Some of the questions you just answered are questions that you've been avoiding asking yourself for a very long time. Each one of the questions you just answered should begin to give you insight into your financial habits and what you're going to learn in *The Commissioner.*

The 10 questions you just answered can be distilled down to four main points. And those points translate into the four goals for this book.

1. **You will learn how to budget the right way.** If you've been reluctant to budget in the past because of your ability to control your income, then you need to understand that budgeting is the key to your long-term financial success. Budgeting will take all the yo-yoing out of your financial life. Yo-yoing describes the up-and-down nature of both financial fortune and financial misfortune.

2. **You will learn how to pay yourself a salary.** Once you have a grip on your expenses and they are properly honed, then you will craft a salary to fit your financial life. No more income ups and downs. Your salary will allow you to pay your bills, save money, and get out of debt.

3. **You will learn how to decrease financial stress and maintain a healthy level of financial wellness.** Stress will pop up in your financial life from time to time. You can't fully eliminate it, but you can learn to diminish it and diminish its impact. This is where the concept of financial wellness comes in. Just like with your health, a general sense and understanding of wellness can make challenging times a bit easier.

4. **You will learn how to build wealth.** Wealth comes to people who make the best use of the resources they are given. It's hard to generate true wealth when you judge your self-worth by last month's sales. It's common for salespeople to dream about giant quarters and great years in order to generate wealth. But wealth is best created with a strategy, not just a dream of having a good year. You will learn how to best harness both money and time.

CHAPTER 2

DEBT

One of the most common financial and coping tools used by commission income-earners is debt. People who want or need to smooth out the bumps of variable income may utilize a credit card or credit line to do so. If you step away from the stress of the situation and break down the elements, you'll quickly see there's a better way.

As a commission income-earner, what is debt's function when you don't have enough income during a particular period? It's a cash influx that patches a hole. People often rationalize the borrowing by intending to repay the debt when a more robust income period arrives. If you created a physical representation of this event, it would look like Figure 2.1.

The yo-yoing nature of Figure 2.1 brings a tremendous amount of financial stress and creates the feeling of never being able to get ahead. It may seem like a good idea to wipe out debts when a bigger income month arrives, but a more measured approach is more appropriate. You want to repay debts in a way that keeps your momentum heading the right direction, not oscillating back and forth between positive and negative. Figure 2.2 represents the better way to vanquish accumulated debt.

YOUR RELATIONSHIP WITH DEBT

How do you view debt? This is a big but important question. I've encountered many salespeople who view debt as a bridge to a lifestyle they feel entitled to. That's not necessarily as negative as it may seem, but it's not great, either.

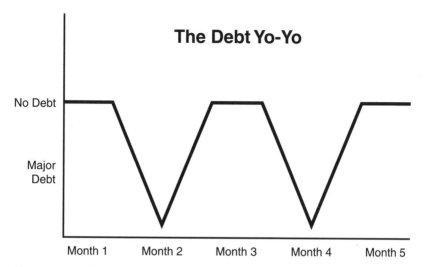

Figure 2.1 The wrong way.

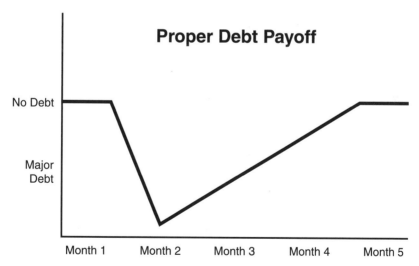

Figure 2.2 The right way.

Let's not be obtuse and suggest that all debt is bad. Debt exists in a person's life for several reasons. It may exist due to a lack of preparedness. It may exist due to poor behavior and decision-making. And it may exist as a reasonable strategy. But no matter the reason, debt consistently does one not-so-good thing: It obligates you to your past. In fact, every time you make the decision to go into debt, your current self is creating a relationship with your future self. It's hard enough to fund both your current lifestyle and your future life. If you throw in a relationship with your past financial decisions, then watch out.

When you're on a commission or variable income, paying down debt or rectifying your financial past can be one of the biggest causes of struggle. I've seen commission-income people aggressively try to pay off debt, just to find themselves back into debt when their income starts to suffer again. Why? Because they've got a yo-yo problem.

Let's talk about Janet, a veteran realtor. Her annual revenue for the past five years has been in excess of $98,000. While her earnings have been beyond commendable, she has been dealing with somewhere between $5,000 and $15,000 of credit card debt over the same timeframe. Upon earning a large sum of money at the closing table, Janet will aggressively attack her debt. But within two months, she's right back in debt trouble again.

Janet has a major yo-yo problem. A yo-yo problem is when you use "good months" to pay down debt, but then the "bad months" take you right back into debt. It's not only frustrating, but it can stifle your financial progress for years. Here's the good news: It's 100 percent avoidable.

Janet thinks she has a debt problem. She doesn't. Debt isn't a debt problem; it's a cash-flow problem. The minimum payment for each of your debts occupies your income. In other words, debt creates monthly obligations. The goal in paying down debt is to eliminate these obligations. If you take a large chunk of cash that's otherwise needed for living expenses and throw it at debt, then you will create a future debt problem. The key to debt reduction while on a commission or variable income is to pay it down systematically while reducing your living expenses.

This requires a heck of a strategy when you are on a *fixed* income. If you're on a variable income, you'll need a great debt-reduction strategy and—more importantly—an income stabilization strategy. The whole point of *The Commissioner* is to stabilize your income, but for now let's just focus on learning the proper debt-reduction strategy.

Janet needs to switch her debt repayment strategy to the momentum method.

TYPES OF DEBT

There are several different types of debt, and many of them have unique characteristics. It's imperative that you know how each type of debt works, the truths surrounding the debts, and where the type of debt falls on the Good Debt/Bad Debt scale.

The Good Debt/Bad Debt scale is an admittedly subjective scale on which you can begin to measure the utility of each different type of debt. A 1 on the Good Debt/Bad Debt scale indicates that there is close to zero sense in having or holding that type of debt. A 5 on the scale indicates that you're properly leveraging debt to improve your overall financial standing. I'm not going to go so far as to say there are good debts. But I will admit some debts are relatively better to hold than others.

For instance, I think a mortgage is the best debt to have, on a relative basis. But I'd rather you not have a mortgage at all. I don't really care about deducting the mortgage interest on your taxes. If you didn't have a mortgage payment, then your cash flow would still net positive compared to having a mortgage payment and deducting the mortgage interest on your taxes.

Consider this: If your gross household income is $80,000 and you pay $5,000 in mortgage interest, then your taxable income will become $75,000, after you've claimed the mortgage interest deduction on your tax return. Now, let's say you have a marginal tax rate of 25 percent. Your mortgage interest deduction just saved you $1,250 in taxes. I've got to admit, that's pretty awesome. You paid $5,000 in interest and reduced your taxes by $1,250, for a net outflow of $3,750. Let's now consider the alternative.

If you don't have any mortgage interest to deduct, your taxable income will remain $80,000. You don't get to legally avoid $1,250 in taxes, but you also don't have to pay $5,000 in mortgage interest. Whereas having mortgage interest to deduct (in our previous example) results in a net cash outflow of $3,750, having no mortgage interest to deduct results in a net cash outflow of $0. The choice is simple. If you keep a mortgage so that you can deduct the interest, you will pay a net amount of $3,750. If you don't have a mortgage, you will pay nothing.

The "keeping a mortgage to deduct the interest expense" myth is an example of trying to out-math math. And you can't out-math math.

We will discuss the proper way to pay off your debts later in this chapter, but you should feel especially compelled to pay off your debts that fall on the low end of the Good Debt/Bad Debt scale. That being said, don't be dismissive of the debts you have on the top end of the Good Debt/Bad Debt scale.

STUDENT LOANS

Seventy-one percent of college seniors who graduated in 2013 had student loans. The average balance of the student loans was roughly $30,000. Student loans are available either through the federal government or through your university/college, bank, or credit union, usually as part of a financial-aid package. Designed to help you pay off expenses related to education, student loans differ slightly from traditional loans in that they're often offered at a lower interest rate. And, unlike most types of loans, you may have the option to defer your student-loan payment until after graduation.

Student loans are among the most substantial types of debt for recent college graduates. According to a study cited in *The Wall Street Journal*, over the last decade the average student-loan debt in the United States has increased significantly—from roughly $18,000 in 2004 to $33,000 in 2014. The percentage of students graduating with debt has also risen from 64 percent in 2004 to 71 percent in 2014.[1]

---

[1] http://blogs.wsj.com/numbers/congatulations-to-class-of-2014 -the-most-indebted-ever-1368.

There are substantial differences between federal, sometimes called *subsidized*, student loans and private student loans. You need to understand what type of loans you have and how their characteristics affect your strategy to pay them off.

Federal (subsidized) student loans

▶ You don't need a credit check to obtain federal student loans. Yet these loans can help you establish healthy credit.

▶ The nature of a subsidized loan is that the government will pay the interest payments on the loan for students with financial needs while the borrower is still at least a half-time student.

▶ You don't have a cosigner on your federal loans.

▶ You don't have to start repaying your federal loans until you are no longer classified as a student (you graduate, leave school, or switch to being less than a half-time student).

▶ Interest rates are fixed and are generally lower than the rates on private student loans.

Private student loans

▶ No one pays the interest on private student loans but you. There are no interest subsidies.

▶ Interest rates are variable and can approach 20 percent.

▶ Many private student loans require you to start making payments while you are still in school.

▶ You have to qualify for private loans via your credit score or a cosigner.

Good Debt/Bad Debt rating: 4

Analysis: One of the main considerations in your decision to take on student-loan debt was the possibility of an increased income due to a higher level of education and functional aptitude. If you played your cards right (and took out the right amount of debt for the quality and relevance of education purchased), then you made an investment in your future. In essence, you leveraged debt properly. And while your decision to borrow money was potentially both wise and admirable, you should still be diligent in your efforts to pay it back.

While many student-loan programs will allow you 25 years to repay your debts, you shouldn't take this long. Ten years is the standard loan-repayment period for a reason. Get your education and then pay it off. Don't live with student-loan debt for a quarter century just because you are allowed to.

BANK CREDIT CARD DEBT

Consumer credit tools can be traced back to the 1800s, when oil companies and general merchants extended credit to their individual consumers. It wasn't until the 1960s that a national system for accepting credit cards was implemented. The companies we now know as MasterCard and Visa were among the trailblazers of the consumer credit industry.

Credit cards are more prevalent today than ever before. This increased usage has led to a treasure trove of problems. High interest rates, penalties, and fees associated with your credit cards can quickly add up. Based on analysis of data provided by the Federal Reserve, the average American household owes

$15,480 in credit card debt. The average college graduate owes close to $3,000.[2]

While many people might tell you that it's important to increase your credit score while you're in college and right after by using your credit cards early and often, it's much more important to focus on your financial health, not some arbitrary score that can take you down a nasty path. In fact, your credit score, that mystical metric that is often pointed to as the bastion of financial wellness, isn't a very good indicator of your financial health. Net worth, which is your assets minus your liabilities, paints a much clearer picture. Wouldn't you rather reduce your debts and increase your savings than manipulate an overrated number that just proves you are good at borrowing?

The good news is that a 2013 study by Fidelity suggested that credit card debt among recent college graduates is in decline. The 2009 Credit Card Reform Act is to blame for this. Or maybe I should say it's to credit for this. College students can no longer be offered freebies on campus for opening up a credit card.

You'll notice that our discussion on credit cards will continue throughout this book. This is purposeful, the opposite of subtle, and the biggest hint you have ever been given.

Good Debt/Bad Debt rating: 1

Analysis: Why? Why do it? You don't need to. Save money, and then use the money to buy stuff you want. Don't borrow and

[2] http://www.nerdwallet.com/blog/credit-card-data/average-credit-card-debt-household.

then find a way to pay for it later. When you do that, you will end up paying more for your purchases. And for you "pay off your credit card at the end of each month" people, I've got a little something for you later in the book.

STORE CREDIT CARD DEBT

Nearly every major retailer—from Gap to Amazon to Walmart—offers customers the opportunity to apply for a credit card that can be used only in their store. They lure customers into signing up for their cards with an interest-free grace period (usually the first six months) or a discount on their purchases.

Consumers get into trouble when they neglect to pay off their balances—or when they use their cards beyond the interest-free grace period. Store credit cards offer high interest rates, many of them right around 25 percent. It doesn't take long for an interest rate that high to wreak havoc on someone's financial health. In addition, they do little to impact your credit score, and they have low limits, putting you at risk for added fees.

Store credit cards exist for one simple reason: to sell you more stuff. Every deal, coupon, or special offer is designed to induce spending, not help you. Store credit programs are created under the guise of loyalty programs, but who is being loyal to whom? In nearly every extreme debt situation I have ever encountered, store credit cards are present. They are a financial gateway drug.

Your best bet is to avoid store credit cards altogether. Signing up for a card to defer payment for an item over six months is a good indication that you shouldn't be buying that item in the first place.

Good Debt/Bad Debt rating: 1

Analysis: Store credit cards are as unnecessary as they are dangerous. They aren't collector cards. If your wallet has space for six credit cards, buy a smaller wallet. Don't fill up the wallet with store credit cards. Oh, and don't buy the wallet using a credit card.

CAR LOAN

Unless you live in the heart of a major city and have access to safe and affordable mass transit, chances are you're going to have to buy a car. While a car is arguably a necessity in the twenty-first century, it doesn't mean you have to disregard sensibility and contribute to the growing trend of skyrocketing car loans.

According to Experian Automotive, which tracks millions of auto loans written each quarter, the average amount borrowed by new car buyers in the fourth quarter of 2013 was a record-high $27,430. The average monthly payment for a new car was $471, and the average monthly payment for a used-car loan was $352.[3]

To make matters even worse, a record 20 percent of new-car loans were extended beyond six years. A car is one of the worst investments you can make. It depreciates in value immediately after you drive it off the lot and continues to depreciate for the duration of the time you own it. Borrowing money to buy a depreciating asset isn't a great idea. By the mere fact that there is an interest charge associated with the loan, you are paying

---

[3] http://www.cnbc.com/id/101461972#.

more for a car than it's worth, and when you have paid it off, it's worth even less.

Good Debt/Bad Debt rating: 3

Analysis: It's not the end of the world if you have car debt, but it's also not the best idea. If you ever find yourself underwater on a car (meaning you owe more on the car than it's worth), don't trade in the car and finance the entire process. You will owe more on your new car than it's worth, and your new car will instantly depreciate even further when you take it off the lot. Again, just because a car dealer will let you borrow $40,000 on a $30,000 car doesn't mean you should do it.

HOME LOAN (MORTGAGE)

At some point, you'll more than likely consider buying your first home. Home ownership is, after all, part of the American Dream. Home ownership is also the number-one reason why many Americans carry the burden of debt for the majority of their lives.

The type of mortgage you get is incredibly important. A mortgage can be a decent use of debt because the underlying asset (the house) is, generally speaking, an appreciating asset. An appreciating asset is an asset that goes up in value over time. So by the time you have paid off your mortgage, the home itself generally, but not always, will have increased in value.

Good Debt/Bad Debt rating: 5

Analysis: A home is an asset that is easily exchanged in a reasonable marketplace. You don't necessarily have to wait until the end of your mortgage term to profit on the buying and selling of a house. Of any debt you could ever possibly acquire, this is the best one. But remember, we're comparing a mortgage to the likes of credit cards and payday loans.

MEDICAL DEBT

Rising medical costs and insurance premiums have made medical debt the number-one cause of bankruptcy filings in the United States, according to a recent study from NerdWallet Health. More than 1.7 million Americans will file bankruptcy because of unpaid medical bills in the next year, and 56 million adults—more than 20 percent of the population between 19 and 64—will struggle with medical debt. In an attempt to pay off their debt, more than 11 million people will increase their credit card debt as well.

While preparing for medical debt can be difficult—especially as a young person at the peak of his or her physical health—building up a significant emergency savings fund and funding a Health Savings Account (HSA), when applicable, can help offset the financial repercussions of medical expenses.

Anecdotally, medical debt has always seemed to me to be the most ignored. I've witnessed a great number of people exhibit outright dismissive attitudes about medical debt.

Good Debt/Bad Debt rating: 4

Analysis: While you shouldn't carry medical debt, if you happen to acquire some due to medical issues, you shouldn't panic. Your health is very important, and if you make wise health-care decisions, you can feel justified in spending money on improving your health. Medical debt tends to bring quite a bit of stress, because of the residual stress associated with the root medical problem. Do not interpret a rating of 4 on the Good Debt/Bad Debt scale as justification to ignore your medical debts. However, if there is a debt about which you truly don't have a choice, it's medical debt. Take it seriously.

LINES OF CREDIT (SECURED AND UNSECURED)

A line of credit is different from a loan in that it's not one lump sum of money. Instead, you can draw from a specified amount of money in your line of credit in the same way that you would use a credit card. There are two types of lines of credit: secured and unsecured.

A secured line of credit is one that is backed by collateral, such as a house or another piece of property. An unsecured line of credit is one that has no collateral backing it up. Because unsecured lines of credit are riskier for lenders, their interest rates are significantly higher than secured lines of credit.

Both are risky for borrowers, and for different reasons. If you can't pay back your secured line of credit, you put yourself at risk of losing whatever collateral you've offered up. If you can't pay back your unsecured line of credit, high interest rates can add up quickly. Be very careful when tapping a line of credit, which can certainly have a blank-check quality to it.

It's not uncommon for homeowners to tap their equity line of credit to make home improvements. Sometimes the home improvements increase the underlying property value, and sometimes they don't. You've heard it a million times, and in case you haven't, let me say it again: Your house is not a piggy bank. Removing equity from your home, even to theoretically increase the value of your home via home-improvement projects, is a bad idea. Home-improvement projects very rarely equal a dollar-for-dollar increase in home value. That $15,000 landscaping job you just completed probably did close to nothing for the value of your home.

Good Debt/Bad Debt rating: 2

Analysis: It's only fair that I present a reasonable alternative to home-equity loans. In fact, I'm going to suggest something that I personally did for a major home-improvement project we completed last spring: Save the money for the project. Saving money for a major financial goal is substantially more productive than funding a financial goal with borrowed money.

It's the difference between a store credit card and layaway. Layaway has gotten a weird reputation over the past couple of decades, but why? Layaway employs delayed gratification, while putting a purchase on a credit card employs instant gratification. Which is better? Frankly, delayed gratification is better, because instant gratification funded by debt is dangerous.

PAYDAY LOANS

Payday loans are loans given against your paycheck by a third-party lender. For example, if you have bills that need to be paid on Monday but you won't be paid until Friday, you can provide employment records and proof of an income stream to a lender and take out a payday loan—complete with a borrowing fee—to get the money faster.

Payday loan lenders are banking (literally) on the notion that you will turn into a repeat borrower. That's when the high interest rates of payday loans compound and lead to a vicious cycle of borrowing. In a recent report from the Consumer Financial Protection Bureau, more than 80 percent of payday loans are either rolled into a new loan or followed by an additional loan within 14 days.[4] If there ever was a predatory loan, this is it.

I have seen low-income earners get mixed up in the payday loan game, and surprisingly enough, I've seen high-income earners get mixed up in the payday loan game. And in both instances, the end result is awful. There are payday loans with 1,000 percent interest rates. That's not a fictitious number; that's a real number. Don't do it. You're better than that. In fact, everyone is better than that. One-thousand percent interest rate!

Good Debt/Bad Debt rating: 1

Analysis: One-thousand percent interest rate!

---

[4] http://www.washingtonpost.com/business/the-trap-of-payday-loans-can-lead-to-triple-digit-interest-rates/2014/03/25/ca1853dc-b471-11e3-8cb6-284052554d74_story.html.

PERSONAL LOANS (FROM A FINANCIAL INSTITUTION)

A personal loan is an unsecured loan (meaning that you don't have to put up any collateral) granted for personal use. You might secure a personal loan to help pay for everything from medical expenses to replacing your home's air conditioner to covering college costs.

The loan amount is determined by your credit history and your income—essentially, your ability to pay back your lender. Because no collateral is involved, your interest rates will be much higher.

Good Debt/Bad Debt rating: 2

Analysis: It's possible you will need to take a personal loan from a bank, but you should try to avoid it. A personal loan is similar to a secured or an unsecured equity line, except a personal loan isn't open ended and can have a shorter amortization schedule.

PERSONAL LOANS (FROM A FAMILY MEMBER OR FRIEND)

Do you love your family and friends? (The correct answer is yes.) Then why make your financial problems their financial problems? Personal loans from family and friends, whether formal or informal, are a bad idea. If a lending institution isn't willing to loan you money because of your credit-(un)worthiness, why subject your loved ones to your objectively high level of lending risk?

Your family and friends may offer to help you out financially, but unless it's life or death, say no. Relationships should not be splintered for avoidable financial reasons.

Good Debt/Bad Debt rating: 1

Analysis: Avoid both sides of the personal loans from friends or family equation. You will almost always come away disappointed.

TAX DEBT

Tax debt happens when you fail to pay earned income taxes to the state or federal government. In addition to the debt total, depending on the severity of the situation, you could incur fines and penalties (including jail time) for delayed payments.

If tax debt goes unpaid for long enough, the IRS has the right to garnish your wages until the debt is paid off. You might also have the ability to set up a payment plan with the IRS to pay off your debt in installments.

The moral of the story? Make sure you know how to calculate your personal and business taxes—or hire someone who can. That investment will more than offset the costs incurred from tax debt. You want stress? Owe the IRS back taxes. You want to avoid financial stress? Start by keeping current with your taxes. You don't want to go down the tax-debt road. It's a dead end.

Good Debt/Bad Debt rating: 1

Analysis: Did you read the part of this section that said jail time? Jail time is an automatic 1 on the Good Debt/Bad Debt rating scale.

COLLECTION DEBT

If you are unable to pay a bill, the lender can send it directly to a debt-collection agency. As a result, you'll begin to receive phone calls and letters from collectors in the weeks following your first missed payment. If you owe a substantial amount of money, debt collectors can take extreme measures—such as filing judgments—to ensure that you repay the debt.

Being unable to pay a bill is stressful in the first place; being sent to collections adds another level of financial stress that can affect your entire life.

Good Debt/Bad Debt rating: 1

Analysis: A strange yet common reaction to having debt go to collections is to ignore the collection calls. Don't ignore the collection calls. Unfortunately, when a debt goes to collections, you will lose leverage. The collection agents are generally compensated based on the amount of money they can collect from you. To move on with your financial life, you must right things with the collection companies that hold your debts. Don't let it get this far—but if it does, deal with it quickly.

JUDGMENTS

Judgments are legal obligations to pay a debt or damages that have been issued in a court of law. If a creditor takes you to court and is awarded a judgment, it gives the creditor the right to use additional methods to collect the debt they are owed, including wage garnishment, liens, and levies.

Wage garnishment involves an automatic deduction from your paycheck—up to 25 percent—each pay period. This money is sent directly to your judgment creditor until the debt is paid off.

When a lien is placed on your home or your property, you will have to pay the debt with the money you earn from selling or refinancing the assets that have liens.

If the judgment creditor is awarded a levy, they can take funds directly from your checking or savings account—or even levy your personal property and sell it in an auction—to pay off the debt.

Good Debt/Bad Debt rating: 2

Analysis: Look, judgments aren't great. And I understand that having your wages garnished is both frustrating and embarrassing, but at least you'll get out of debt. Don't get me wrong; you should avoid letting your debts get so out of control that a judge is involved, but there is a silver lining to having your debts go to judgment: You will finally deal with the obligation you've been fighting or ignoring. You can't make progress when you're in denial. A judgment flips the denial switch to reality.

DEBT PAY-DOWN PROCESS

People use three primary strategies to pay off debt. One of these strategies is effective; the other two strategies are commonly used yet often fall short. You must understand all three strategies, which we'll discuss in a moment, to understand why one strategy is the best.

Paying down debt is challenging for several reasons, but the two hardest parts are your battle against human nature and your simultaneous attack of your financial past, present, and future.

Before you get started with your debt pay-down, you must understand a very important piece of the debt-reduction puzzle: You must stop using debt as a tool. It's impossible to get out of debt if you keep trickling back into debt each month by using your credit card. Stop using your bank credit card, store credit card, and/or line of credit. You won't be able to stay afloat if there's a hole in your boat.

Your commitment not to use debt as a tool will require sacrifice. Your credit card may have allowed you to buy some time in the past, but the time you bought came at a serious price. Now it's time to pay the piper.

Once you've committed to not using your credit cards, you are ready to get out of debt. The three most popular methods of paying off debt are the *math* method, the *momentum* method, and the *shotgun* method. Do you know which one is best?

THE MATH METHOD

Because debt deals with numbers, you'd think math would and should be involved in paying off debt. Well, it is, but at some point it makes sense to ignore the math and focus on your behavior instead. We'll talk more about that in a bit.

To be fair, the math method is technically the best way to pay off debt. But I find it to be much less effective than other methods. The reality is, if you were so good at operating in purely mathematical terms, would you have all that debt in the first place? Probably not.

When using the math method of paying off debt, you focus on attacking the debt that has the highest interest rate. Each debt that you have has its own interest rate. Some of your debts may have interest rates less than 10 percent, some in excess of 10 percent, and some interest rates even skyrocket past 30 percent. The higher the interest rate, the more money you will end up paying your creditors if you continue to stay in debt to them. This higher borrowing cost over time causes many people to attack their debts with the highest interest rates first. And technically, they are doing the right thing. The faster they pay down the high-interest debts, the less interest they'll pay on those debts. It's textbook perfect. But human nature is a fickle beast.

Paying off your past financial decisions can prove so difficult and time consuming that you may abandon a successful strategy if you don't feel you're getting the results you desire in a timely manner. Behavior change needs to be reinforced. If you've shifted your financial habits to throw more money toward your debts, you want to see tangible, powerful results, right? Consider the following scenario.

You have two $2,000 debts. One is a car loan at 2.9 percent interest, and the other debt is a credit card at 29.99 percent interest. Which debt would you focus on paying off first? When I say "focus on," I mean paying more than the minimum required payment.

For this example, let's assume you have an additional $200 per month you could put toward one of your debts. If you used the highest interest rate method, you would attack the credit card, because its rate is 27.09 percent more than the car loan interest rate. But what do you think the minimum payment is for the credit card? Maybe $70 or so? Now, what do you think the payment on the car loan is? For the sake of the example, let's say $300. If you were to pay off the car loan first, you would free up $300 per month of cash flow. If you were to pay off the high-interest credit card first, you'd free up $70 per month of cash flow.

By ignoring the interest rates, you would be able to access $300 faster than you could access $70. Additionally, if you had been paying the $200 extra toward your car loan, then you would have been making $500 payments. You would already be used to living without the $500 with regard to discretionary spending, so you could simply start paying $570 per month toward your credit card balance once your car loan was paid off.

And just like that, you've dipped your toe into the waters of the momentum method....

THE MOMENTUM METHOD

The momentum method of paying off debt has been around for years, and people call it many different things. I call it the momentum method. It takes advantage of human behavior and engagement. Many people give up on their debt-repayment strategy because they don't see the fruits of their labor. The momentum method ensures that you will see your debts start to shrink in a dramatic and impactful way.

In a nutshell, the momentum method requires you to make minimum payments on all your debts, except your smallest-balance debt. You should then aggressively attack the smallest-balance debt, paying as much toward it as possible. Once it's eliminated, take its minimum payment and use it to focus on the next smallest debt, along with all the other income you've dedicated to debt repayment. Continue attacking the smallest-balance debt until all your debts are eliminated.

I prefer the momentum method and fully endorse it. I'll fully explain how it works after you understand the shotgun method.

THE SHOTGUN METHOD

Shotguns are effective because when you pull the trigger once, your target area is riddled with shot. The idea is that by peppering the target area, you are more likely to hit the intended specific target. A rifle, on the other hand, gives you one shot to hit the intended target. Yet from a distance, a rifle is a much more powerful weapon. Don't spray your debt from a distance with lots of little pellets.

The shotgun method of debt is when you attack many debts at once. Specifically, you pay more than the minimum payment on several different debts. I know you've always heard that you *should* pay more than your minimum payments on all your different debts, but you shouldn't. You will get out of debt much faster if you focus all of your extra payments toward your lowest-balance debt.

People who use the shotgun method often describe a sensation of running in place. A few years ago I met a nurse who was paying extra on all her different debts. She had nine credit cards, a car loan, and three medical bills. She was paying $1,500 per month toward her debts, yet she hadn't made much progress in more than two years. Upon discovering that she was using the shotgun method, we changed her strategy to the momentum method and ran some quick projections. In just two short months using the momentum method, she paid off five debts and freed up $450 of cash flow per month.

GETTING OUT OF DEBT

Eliminating a debt means eliminating a minimum payment. The faster you eliminate a debt, the faster you get to recapture its minimum payment. Because of this, your goal is to pay off debts as quickly as possible. The fastest way to do this is to attack the smallest-balance debt first. Here's how it works.

STEP 1: MAP OUT YOUR DEBT

Before you decide how you're going to pay off your debt, you need to figure out what debt you actually have. If you are in a bit of denial over your debts, you may have never compiled a comprehensive list. To do this, list all of your debts, from the smallest balance to the largest balance, in Table 2.1. Allow yourself as much time as necessary to complete this table—and make sure not to leave out any details. Remember to list every type of debt. This includes credit cards, mortgages, car loans, student loans, personal loans, and even debts that have made their way to collections.

STEP 2: BUILD MOMENTUM WITH SMALL DEBT VICTORIES

Don't make equal payments on each debt; it's inefficient. Employing this strategy may have been your problem for years. It's not unusual for people to pay extra on all their debts. As you know, your debts have a required minimum payment. Many people do what they believe to be a good idea and pay more than the minimum payment on all their debts. Frustration eventually sets in because they don't appear to be making any progress toward their goal of being debt free.

Instead, you should focus on paying off your smallest debt and getting the balance down to zero. This will free up the money you were putting toward the monthly minimum payment so you can put it toward the next debt—not to mention it also helps you create a sense of financial momentum. You may start out by paying only $100 per month extra above the minimum payment. But by the end of the debt pay-down process, you might actually be putting upwards of $1,000 per month toward the next lowest debt balance. This scenario is possible because you have eliminated debts and are able to use former minimum payments to help you pay off the next debt.

If you're wondering why we're focusing on the lowest balance instead of the highest interest rate, it's because we're trying to create momentum and zero balances. So at this point, try not to concern yourself with the interest rates (even though I know that goes against conventional wisdom).

Creating small victories and zero balances up front is the financial equivalent of losing that first five pounds on a diet. You just need some confirmation that what you're doing really

Table 2.1: Map Out Your Debt			
Whom Do You Owe?	Amount Owed	Minimum Payment	New Monthly Payment

Table 2.1: Map Out Your Debt

Whom Do You Owe?	Amount Owed	Minimum Payment	New Monthly Payment

works. As you pay off these balances, you'll begin to accumulate the money you were once putting toward minimum payments each month, allowing you to apply those savings to the next lowest balance on your list.

STEP 3: COMMIT TO A DEBT-PAYMENT SCHEDULE

This process is as simple as it gets, assuming you commit to making it part of your routine. The key is to keep chipping away at the debt. Sure, it will take time, but it will also work. Every time you free up money in your budget, apply it to your next lowest balance.

As a personal finance expert, I'm always tempted to create complicated processes for debt liquidation. But the reality is you need a very simple plan that's easy to stick to. Debt liquidation is way too important to complicate it with confusing financial algorithms and impossible goals.

YOUR PERSPECTIVE NEEDS TO SHIFT

There's no doubt your debt is a hindrance. But if you shift your perspective, then this hindrance immediately becomes a legitimate opportunity. This isn't some sort of strange exercise in semantics. If you pay down your debt between now and your retirement date, it may actually put you in a better position over those who are spending a vast majority of their pre-retirement income on consumer habits that have been formed for a decade or more. Whereas those people are forcing themselves to quit a learned habit, you are employing brilliant, healthy habits as you head into your retirement.

People often take on debt payments based on consumer confidence. When your world is great, when the economy is singing and the market is climbing, most people feel confident. Confidence is a great thing, but what generally happens next isn't. Consumer confidence is used as an economic measure for economists because purchasing usually follows it. When confident, a person tends to spend money, not save money. When people lack confidence, they save money. I know; it's a terribly backward way of thinking. Don't waste confidence on creating more obligations. Harness confidence to improve your life, not your lifestyle.

WHAT NOW?

The fewer obligations you have, the less pressure you will put on your income. Your goal is to permanently eliminate as many (debt) obligations as possible. There is a hidden benefit to paying off your debts systematically using the momentum method. You will learn to live without the money you use to pay on your debts' principal and interest each month. The first month you are debt free will determine what's next for you and your financial life.

If, upon becoming debt free, you reabsorb the money you've put toward debt reduction, you'll waste a giant opportunity. The most dangerous month in your financial recovery is always the month after you become debt free, because if you form new habits with your new discretionary income, then you are creating new forms of obligations. Instead, focus on making the best use of your freed-up capital. Strengthen your emergency fund. Increase your contributions to your retirement plan. Do anything to move yourself forward. Don't create new obligations.

CHAPTER 3

BUDGETING

The cardinal sin of a person with a commission income is not knowing his or her household income requirements. A commission income-earner, more than anyone, needs to know exactly how much money needs to be made. Oddly, commission income-earners tend to focus on what they are earning instead of what they *need* to earn to get their financial situation on solid ground.

Probably no group of people hates budgeting more than salespeople. Why? Because budgeting generally is a practice of taking finite resources to handle both fixed and variable expenses. And what do salespeople not have? Finite resources.

Salespeople have infinite resources. The more you sell, the more you earn. It's one of the great things about sales. But the possibility of infinite resources (unlimited income) makes it very difficult to budget. Salespeople often struggle to budget because they don't want to consider their income finite. And what makes things even more challenging is that if salespeople *do* decide to budget, they get into big trouble if they budget based on the wrong income projections.

Let's examine some qualities of great salespeople. You'll find that many of these qualities don't match up with the qualities of good budgeters.

> ▶ **They are confident.** I've yet to meet a great salesperson who isn't confident. This confidence is innate, yet not necessarily based on results. People who are good at budgeting look to the budget to add desired confidence via results. If a person already has confidence, then budgeting can seem unnecessary. However, salespeople's financial confidence is in their ability to create income, not make good financial decisions. It's a common fallacy that people who earn high incomes

somehow know more about money. There is absolutely no correlation between a person's ability to generate income and that same person's ability to make wise financial decisions.

▶ **They are persistent.** Salespeople typically don't take no for an answer. And what is budgeting? It's no for an answer. Can I afford to go on this $10,000 vacation despite my $2,000 in savings? No. Too bad, I'm going. A seasoned salesperson avoids no like the plague. In fact, well-trained salespeople never even ask their customers questions in which no is a potential response.

▶ **They constantly feed the pipeline.** Great salespeople know that there must always be business brewing. With regard to budgeting, this quality creates a mentality of "Don't worry; there's more money coming." That's bad. A person can't disregard a budget because he feels as though he'll have enough money to cover any expense. The goal of budgeting is to make the best use of what's there, not to do whatever you want because you have a hunch more resources are on the way.

▶ **They hold themselves accountable.** A budget is accountability. Self-starters, go-getters, and self-motivated people aren't typically great budgeters. The irony is that many great salespeople thrive under accountability. Accountability is not a bad thing, and salespeople who avoid it don't last very long. Great salespeople hold themselves accountable not only to their company's goals, but to their own goals as well. In this instance, the accountability characteristic matches up perfectly with the concept of budgeting. A budget is simply an accountability system for money.

THE IDEAL HOUSEHOLD BUDGET

You need to understand budgeting not only on a conceptual level, but also on an experiential level. In other words, understanding the *concept* of budgeting isn't enough. You need to actually do it.

The first place to start is by knowing your limits. Unfortunately, many of our big buying decisions are dictated by the people lending us money during those big buying moments. For instance, what a bank will allow you to allocate toward a monthly mortgage payment is much different from what *I* think you should allocate toward a monthly mortgage payment. Their goal is to loan you as much money as they can without causing you to default on your loan. My goal is to encourage you to borrow an amount of money that will still allow you to live a fruitful financial life. That's a pretty big difference.

As you study the ideal household budget in Figure 3.1, compare your current spending percentages with the recommended percentages. We are talking about take-home pay—or net pay, as it's more formally called. Net pay is what you take home after taxes, benefit deductions, and retirement plan contributions.

HOUSING: 25 PERCENT

Nothing—and I mean *nothing*—can ruin your sales career in a more subversive way than a giant house payment. When sales are great, a high mortgage payment seems like it can make

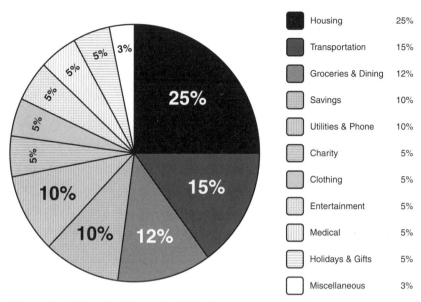

■	Housing	25%
■	Transportation	15%
■	Groceries & Dining	12%
■	Savings	10%
▦	Utilities & Phone	10%
■	Charity	5%
■	Clothing	5%
▦	Entertainment	5%
▦	Medical	5%
▤	Holidays & Gifts	5%
□	Miscellaneous	3%

Figure 3.1 The ideal household budget.

sense. When sales grind to a halt, a high mortgage payment is the catalyst for financial stress.

There's a hint of irony to this: Your house and/or mortgage were sold to you via a sales process. Hopefully you limited the mortgage payment to 25 percent of your monthly income. But it's quite possible you were sold a mortgage and/or home that you couldn't really afford. Just because a bank loans you money, that doesn't mean you can really afford the home you're purchasing. This is a very common problem—and an extraordinarily huge problem for salespeople on commission.

Our natural inclination is to buy as much house as we are allowed, and that is cruel. In many ways, it's much like eating at an all-you-can-eat buffet. The foolish part of our bodies, wherever it may be, convinces us that more is better. But it's not. More can be hell. I'd actually argue that "more is better" has become the American Way. Oddly enough, I believe that more *is* better, just not in the way you'd think.

What do you want more of? This is an essential question, especially for prospective homeowners. Prospective homeowners generally are thinking about housing when they set out to buy a house. But it's foolish for that to be *all* they think about. Buying a house is a tremendously big deal. In many instances, it's the single largest purchase you will ever make. Yet it's rarely treated that way. It's quite strange how we got here, but somewhere along the way, our homes became disproportionately important to us.

I probably don't need to explain why our homes are such an emotional entity, but I will. Our homes are the epicenters of our memories. They keep our children safe; they host meals, parties, prom pictures, and goodbyes. In many ways, our lives wouldn't be complete without a place to host our greatest memories. All of those things can happen anywhere, perhaps for much less than you're currently spending. You will taint your ability to create lovely memories if you make a foolish housing decision. You can prevent this by having the proper focus when making a house decision. That focus? Your life.

Your life isn't about shelter, couches, curtains, square footage, basements, three-car garages, or corner lots. Your life is about everything other than your house: food, vacations, education, family, entertainment, and a ton of other stuff. You cannot afford to do any of these things or indulge any of your interests if your house payment is a disproportionate share of your household budget. Consider these benchmark numbers for housing.

▶ **40 percent or more of household income committed to housing.** Your margin of error is very slim. You are clinically overhoused. You should seek an immediate solution to this problem, especially if you have a car payment, student-loan debt, and/or other consumer debt. It's nearly impossible to save for the future when this much money is going toward your house payment. It is very unlikely that you have a properly funded emergency fund (three months' expenses).

▶ **26 to 39 percent of household income committed to housing.** You listened to the bank, or you followed the advice of a mortgage calculator. You are spending too much on housing, but it's not a fatal error. If you lack a car payment and significant debt, then you should be fine. If you have a car payment or debt, then you are at risk of hating your financial life for a long time.

▶ **25 percent of household income committed to housing.** You precious creature. You listened to Pete the Planner's ideal budget, or you're an otherwise intelligent person. Life is manageable, fruitful, and comfortable when you can limit your house payment to 25 percent of your income. You can get the best of both worlds: a nice home and a nice payment.

▶ **Less than 25 percent of household income committed to housing.** Do you want everything and are willing to sacrifice a foolish housing decision in order to get it? Awesome. Then spend less than 25 percent of your household income on a house payment. Travel the world. Dine out. Drive a sweet ride. Collect wine. You can do these things when you don't over-commit to ridiculous housing costs.

Furthermore, if your mortgage or rent payment, combined with your transportation costs (car payment, insurance, gas), is more than 55 percent of your household income, then we've officially figured out why you're hating life right now.

Show restraint when making a housing decision. You'll actually be able to live a life you want to live.

TRANSPORTATION: 15 PERCENT

Among all of the tricky spending categories, you'll find transportation costs. Car payments, car insurance, and gas seem financially innocuous; in reality, they're anything but. There are more ways to mess up your financial life with poor transportation cost decisions than with decisions in almost any other spending category. You can buy the wrong car, pay too much for it, finance it the wrong way, and then pick the wrong company to insure it. All the while, you are trying to keep your final monthly expenditure under the prescribed 15 percent of your monthly take-home pay. A poor car-buying (or leasing) decision can leave you in a lurch for years.

Staying under budget can be challenging, especially if you have two car payments, as was the case with Tyler and Monique. To compound their issues, Tyler had owed more money on his previous car than it was worth, and he decided to trade it in anyway. Therefore, he did something very common yet very dangerous: He financed negative equity. In other words, he rolled his old loan into his new car loan and essentially paid $34,000 for a $28,000 car. Anecdotally, I've noticed that once people start down this borrowing-decision path, they stay on this path for at least two cars. While a car dealer may present this process as a solution to a transportation problem, it certainly does create a whole other set of problems. So a solution it is not.

In a perfect world, you'd have no car payments. I've personally enjoyed this phenomenon for years now, and I can tell you that there's nothing better. Yet as crazy as this sounds, always having a car payment might be the solution to a transportation budget issue.

Going over your 15 percent transportation budget can create a major cash-flow crunch that hinders your ability to make financial progress in the other areas of your life. And while it may seem as though it always makes sense to temporarily bite the bullet on a higher monthly payment via a car purchase instead of a car lease agreement, often it does not. If a consumer is struggling with other forms of debt, is paying too much for housing, and/or is paying out the ear for daycare, then finding a very inexpensive lease might be the best financial decision. Yes, despite what you've heard, a car lease might actually save the financial day.

A car lease can make sense if you're in a cash-flow crunch. It is neither a long-term solution nor a blank check to get whatever type of car you want. Preferably, if you're in a cash-flow crunch, you'll just buy a very cheap car for cash, but sometimes that isn't an option. And while I realize that leasing a car isn't technically *great* personal finance advice, it is very *practical* personal finance advice. And the reality is that if you're in a big cash-flow crunch, then you haven't shown the greatest propensity to handle technical personal finance decisions, so some practical real-world advice is warranted.

If you choose to lease, make sure you aggressively clean up your financial life during the term of the lease. If it's a three-year lease, then you've got three years to clean up debt, tighten down spending issues, and build cash reserves. The goal in all of this is to make sure you're not spending more than 15 percent of your income on transportation costs (car payments, fuel, and insurance). Feel free to ignore this advice, but don't come to me when you're upset.

GROCERIES AND DINING OUT: 12 PERCENT

If any category of spending is directly affected by your work life, it's this one. This is especially true if you have an expense account. Spending money frequently and freely—whether it's your money or your employer's money—can form some nasty financial habits.

Humans have an odd relationship with food. So much so that we often express our love of food with one of our most precious resources—money. Your money and your consumption of food can at times be overwhelming. I've seen normal families spend upwards of $1,800 per month on food. I've seen financial lives ruined by food, and I once saw a couple blow through 12 percent of their retirement assets in the first year of retirement because they spent so much money on food.

So what is a person supposed to spend on food? And at what point does your food-spending equal a problem?

According to the ideal household budget, it is reasonable to spend 12 percent of your net (after-tax) household income on food. That number includes groceries, dining out, coffee, fermented beverages, and anything else your mouth might consume. For instance, if your take-home pay is $4,000 per month, then your food budget is $480 per month. Is that reasonable? Maybe. But honestly, the 12 percent is a guide. If you spend more than 12 percent of your income on food, then you need to rob some other area of your life to pay for it. What's it gonna be? Your transportation budget? Your savings? Your clothing budget? I don't really care what other area of your financial life you choose to short, but you must account for each and every percentage point that climbs over 12 percent.

People overindulge with food for one of three reasons. First, there's convenience. Any time you exchange money for time, that's convenience. If you are driving home from your kid's soccer practice and you don't want to take the time make dinner when you get home, then you must exchange money for convenience. Don't want to wake up five minutes earlier to pack your lunch for work? Cool. Just know you'll need to exchange money for convenience. And if you exchange money for time too often, you'll have a big financial problem.

The second reason people struggle with their food budget is because some people view food and beverage as entertainment. For transparency's sake, this is me. While I sometimes spend too much money on food because of a desire for convenience, I often find my food overspending is a product of my desire to be entertained by food. I find a delicious meal prepared by a trained chef to be as entertaining as a concert or a movie. And this is specifically why I move the 5 percent that's allocated to entertainment in my ideal household budget toward food. In other words, I spend 17 percent of my income on food. I obviously surpass the prescribed 12 percent, but I account for this by eliminating my entertainment. Besides, I have two toddlers. Entertainment for me is silence.

The third reason people overspend on food is a bit more intricate. I've found that some people are so health conscious that they will buy only organic and specialty foods. While focusing on a healthy lifestyle is certainly a brilliant idea, destroying your finances in the process is a terrible idea. This is why people with a health-food issue should reallocate the 5 percent that's designated for health and medical in the ideal household budget toward food. But if a person with a health-food overspending issue also has other medical expenses, then more expense categories will need to be reduced. Sometimes our health issues require us to spend more money on food. If this is the case for you, just make sure you find the extra money you need to spend on food somewhere else in your budget.

We want it all. The real problems I see often involve people who want convenience, gourmet food, and the healthiest ingredients on the planet. Idealistically, good for them. Realistically, they are going to have a major financial issue that spans years. Food, although a huge part of our lives and culture, is fleeting. We consume it. It leaves our bodies. And as crass as that might seem, your money might just turn into waste.

SAVINGS: 10 PERCENT

Although you will be accumulating your work income into your commissioner pool, this money isn't your savings account. It's in no way an emergency fund for your home life. The 10 percent of your commissioner income that goes toward this savings account is meant to fund life's little financial emergencies. Flat tire? Use your emergency fund. Sick dog? Use your emergency fund. Your emergency fund will prevent you from being forced to give yourself a raise. Your lack of preparedness should never put pressure on your commissioner income.

Consistently save 10 percent of your income until your emergency fund is full (three months' worth of expenses) and then start putting your 10 percent savings toward your middle bucket. We'll discuss this in length in Chapter 7, "Wealth."

If you have consumer debt, then the 10 percent allocated to savings should actually go toward debt reduction. From a net-worth perspective, which you'll learn more about in Chapter 7, paying down debt and saving money are the same thing. Don't feel pressure to put money in your emergency fund while you're focusing on paying off debt. You can get away with $1,000 or so in your emergency fund while you aggressively attack credit-card debt and the like.

UTILITIES: 10 PERCENT

Utilities are utilities, but that doesn't mean you can't help yourself out when making important spending decisions. Internet access, smartphones, and data plans have changed the boring world of utility bills forever. Our addictions to these new types of utility payments have channeled money away from our savings and investments. Anecdotally, it's not uncommon for someone to pay more for their smartphone data plan than they save for their child's education.

But it's not just the newfangled utility bills that challenge. Our utility bills don't just happen to us; we sign up for them. Often, our utility costs become more than we want them to be when we buy too much house—the side effect of buying too much house is high utility bills. If you made your housing decision during a string of thriving months and have now come back down to a more modest income level, then not only will your mortgage payment continue to be difficult, but the utility payments that support your home will be difficult, too.

CHARITY: 5 PERCENT

Your community will only be as good as your commitment to it. If all of your financial resources are used for your household alone, your community will suffer. When your community suffers, you will suffer. Including charity in a budget is difficult for anyone, but it is important for everyone.

Who said charity costs money? A charitable spirit starts in your mind, not your wallet. If you are waiting to have money before you give, then you will never give. Money is not the determining factor on whether you give; your charitable spirit is. Volunteer, start a canned-food drive, or give stuff you don't use to a charitable organization. Don't just sit there and do nothing.

CLOTHING: 5 PERCENT

What's included in the clothing budget? Everything. Clothes for you. Clothes for your kids. Clothes for your spouse. Workout clothes. Work clothes. Casual clothes. Bridesmaid dresses. Rental tuxes. Dry cleaning. Clothing repairs. Shoes. Handbags. More shoes. You may have been excited by the raw numbers, but the "what's included" section may have brought you back to earth. The first step, in my opinion? You must take care of your current clothing.

MEDICAL: 5 PERCENT

If your health-insurance premiums are deducted from the paycheck you receive from your employer pre-tax, then the 5 percent allocated to medical expenses in the ideal household budget will likely be limited to co-pays, prescription-drug costs, and fitness memberships. If you pay for your health insurance *with* your take-home pay, then this 5 percent allocation must be used for your health-insurance premiums, too. In fact, it's unlikely you'll be able to jam your health-care expenses into 5 percent of your take-home pay.

ENTERTAINMENT: 5 PERCENT

Not to suggest enjoying life isn't important, because it is, but your entertainment expense category should truly form itself around your financial life. If money is tight, stability is nowhere to be found, and ends aren't meeting, then you really shouldn't be spending much money on entertaining yourself—or your children, for that matter. It's not unusual for financially unstable people to spend a tremendous amount of money on their children's entertainment, while their financial life is crumbling.

The entertainment expense category includes travel, hobbies, or any other expense that is pleasure driven. Again, the absence of pleasure isn't the goal; the goal is satisfaction. Satisfaction is deeper than the shallow ilk of pleasure-driven instant gratification.

HOLIDAYS AND GIFTS: 5 PERCENT

Do you want to waste opportunity wrapped in a bow? Blow through your entire margin during the holidays. It happens all the time. The timing of your end-of-the-year bonus isn't a Christmas miracle; it's an arbitrary coincidence created thousands of years ago when humanity needed a calendar. It's easy to trick yourself into thinking that when you're spending money on someone else, it's a justifiable, benevolent decision. It may be, but that's unlikely. If you're spending money on gifts for your immediate family, you're spending money on yourself.

MISCELLANEOUS: 3 PERCENT

This is where sales incomes go to die. The dreaded, mysterious, and foggy miscellaneous spending category can ruin your financial life. Why? Because these are your whims. This is discretionary beyond discretion. You will have miscellaneous expenses, but disorganized, unaccountable people tend to have a ton of miscellaneous expenses.

There are some very legitimate expenses in this category that many reasonable and responsible people will have. The miscellaneous category is your home for life-insurance premiums, disability-insurance premiums, pet expenses, and household items.

THE EXPENSE CATEGORIES YOU DON'T SEE

You probably noticed that some very common expenses weren't part of the ideal household budget. Well, lots of expenses aren't part of the ideal household budget. That's not only okay, it's on purpose. Everyone has expenses that don't fall neatly into line with this pie chart. Our challenge is to make room for these other expenses by reducing our spending in the main categories.

As silly as this is to both write and hear, you shouldn't spend more than 100 percent of your take-home pay. However, it's easier said than done. There are many reasons for this, but spending one's gross income is among the biggest culprits. I've found that people often view their income pre-tax and spend it accordingly. For instance, "I make $100,000 per year; of course I can afford a $500 per month car payment." But our gross incomes have very little to do with our net incomes. Based on the amount of deductions the person in our example may have, his or her take-home (net) pay may be only $4,000 per month—not the $8,333.33 per month that we often convince ourselves $100,000 per year gross generates.

DAYCARE

Daycare costs vary based on where you live. In some communities, daycare will cost you $500 per month. Yet in other communities, $2,000 per month is more appropriate. Fortunately, all-day daycare costs are temporary. Your children will eventually go to school, and your financial life can get back on track—that is, unless you send your children to private school.

EDUCATION

Whether you're dealing with your education expenses or someone else's, you need to make room in your household budget. If you have significant monthly education expenses, you will need to significantly reduce your spending in other areas. One of the most common errors I regularly see in this regard is when a parent decides to put their children through private school. The problem isn't the cost of private school; the problem is that parents often don't reduce spending to properly afford private school. This is especially dangerous as parents begin to prepare for college expenses.

Making something like education a priority is great, but making something a priority means de-prioritizing other areas of one's life. If education is going to require more of your discretionary income than the other areas of your life, then the areas you valued greatly in the past must be compromised. You can't all of a sudden spend more money on education without adjusting the rest of your budget. Sadly, I see this happen quite frequently.

DEBT REDUCTION

Ask 100 people how they're going to find enough money to get out of debt, and 99 of them will look outside of their budget. Fortunately, you don't have to look outside of your budget. Your opportunity to pay down your debt lives within your budget. If you have debt—especially consumer debt, such as credit cards, medical bills, or home equity lines—then you need to budget in debt reduction. You must make your debt payments, including additional money to pay toward the principal of your lowest-balance debt, part of your household budget. Debt gets paid off when you take it seriously and stop addressing it with whatever's left at the end of your month.

Look at the ideal household budget and commit to spending less on the core expense categories so that you can rid yourself of consumer debt for good.

STUDENT LOANS

You bought the education; now it's time to take paying for it seriously. If you are fresh out of school, you should subtract your student-loan payments right off the top of your budget, well before you determine the rest of your expenses. For instance, if your net income is $3,500 per month and your student-loan payments are $450, then you should base the rest of your spending and your ideal household budget on the remaining $3,050.

If you already have established expenses, then your student loans should be included in your debt-reduction plan. Part of the problem with student-loan debt is that graduates tend to downplay the negative impact the loans can have on the financial future. Pay down your student-loan debts just as you would credit-card debts and medical bills.

YOUR BUDGET WILL FORM YOUR SALARY

If you live your life on a variable income, budgeting may seem impossible. It's not. Budgeting makes thriving on a variable income possible. Figure 3.2 contains a table you can use to sketch out your budget.

The reasons to budget are numerous, but the primary reason you need to budget is because as a commissioner, your budget will determine your new salary.

YOUR MONTHLY HOUSEHOLD INCOME			
HOUSING		**TRANSPORTATION**	
Mortgage/Rent		Car Payment A	
Electric		Car Payment B	
Gas		Gasoline	
Phone		Maintenance	
Cell		Auto Insurance	
Cable		License Plates	
Internet		**Total**	
Water			
Waste		**FOOD**	
Lawncare		Groceries	
HOA		Coffee	
Total		Work Lunch	
		Dining Out	
		Total	

Figure 3.2 Your budget.

PERSONAL CARE		EXISTING DEBT	
		(Credit Cards, Student Loans) Not Cars	
Clothing		Debt Payment #1	
Cleaning/Laundry		Debt Payment #2	
Hair Care		Debt Payment #3	
Medical		Debt Payment #4	
Books/Subscriptions		Debt Payment #5	
Entertainment		Debt Payment #6	
Gifts		Debt Payment #7	
Pets		Debt Payment #8	
Total		**Total**	
OTHER			
Savings			
Life			
Insurance			
College Funds			
Total			

BUDGET

TOTAL

Figure 3.2 Your budget.

CHAPTER 4

PAY YOURSELF A SALARY

(33-58)

My request of you is simple yet powerful. I want three months of your undivided attention. I realize this is a big ask. But please understand that in the scope of your entire career, it's basically nothing. Three months of a 25-year career is 1 percent of your career. You can have the other 99 percent to yourself. If we're able to put together a plan in which you give me 1 percent of your career, and I deliver financial stability for the remaining 99 percent of your career, do you think we'd have a basis for doing business together? Sorry. Sometimes I can't shake the salesman out of me. You know what they say: You can take a person out of sales, but you can't take sales out of a person.

In return for committing 1 percent of your career to this book, I will pay you a salary. Well, you will pay yourself a salary. A salary will help you smooth out the rough times and act efficiently in the great times. You will keep more of your income, you will experience less financial stress, and you will become more productive than ever before.

CONSIDERING SEASONALITY, BONUSES, AND OVERTIME

You need to understand several aspects of your particular employment income. Among a bevy of things, you need to know whether there is any real seasonality to your income. Yes! Lots of people think their profession and income are affected by seasonality, yet often the perceived seasonality is a myth. Y/maybe

Early in my career as a financial planner, I was told that people generally only buy life insurance in the fall. Everywhere I went, everything I heard was "people only like buying life insurance in the fall." First of all, no one likes buying life insurance, ever. Second, I came to find out that the company I worked for had a Fall Life Sales Promotion that had been in existence for decades. In other words, people only bought life insurance in the fall because the salespeople in that company were specifically incentivized to sell life insurance in the fall. It was actually quite ridiculous. If you looked at the top salespeople within the organization, none of them gave a hoot about the Fall Life Sales Promotion. These top producers refused to buy into this manufactured seasonality.

Real seasonality can create major challenges, if you don't put together a plan to address it. Professional athletes have income seasonality concerns, as do construction workers and teachers who choose to receive their pay only during the school year. Realtors have long studied and dealt with the ramifications of home buying around the holidays and during winter in cold-weather locales. In all of these instances, proper income planning, which you are about to learn, can mitigate most challenges.

The strange thing about seasonality is that we are all subject to income seasonality on a much more macro scale. We have two seasons in our career: the earning years and the years we aren't earning. Not to work over your blood pressure here, but if you can't navigate micro seasonality, how are you going to navigate your macro seasonality?

You *can* do something about seasonality. Don't let seasonality freak you out, and don't let it materialize into the built-in excuse it appears to be.

Besides identifying seasonality, you need to know how bonus opportunities affect your income, from a time perspective. Are you only getting year-end bonus opportunities? Or do you have the opportunity to earn bonuses throughout the year, in addition to your other variable compensation? If handled incorrectly, bonuses can be become a double-edged sword to your financial life. Once you're dependent on them, they must persist in order to keep you afloat. But if you break your dependence on bonuses, then you take back control of your financial life. And besides, if you need a bonus to survive, then it really isn't a "bonus" to you. Initially in *The Commissioner* system, you will need the bonuses to fund your pool. But after the pool is funded, not only will you break your dependence on your bonuses, but you also will be able to use your bonuses to create a great financial life.

Don't forget about overtime, either. If your compensation plan includes the possibility of overtime, take advantage of it... wisely. Overtime can be dangerous if it increases your break-even point. And from a budgeting perspective, overtime can disappear just as quickly as it can appear, as can all additional income possibilities, such as bonuses. When you take on extra hours, put the additional revenue to work. Revenue? You are about to learn why the money your employer pays you should now be called *revenue,* and the money you pay yourself should be called *income.* I have some explaining to do....

UNDERSTANDING COMPENSATION STRUCTURES

Variable incomes come in all shapes and sizes. Whether you're a waiter who makes below minimum wage hourly and then survives with tips, or you're an outside sales rep who has a $75,000 base salary with commission and bonus potential that could skyrocket you into the $200k range, you need a solid plan for leveling out your income.

It's important to take a moment and make sure you understand how the different types of compensation structures work.

SALARY ONLY

A salary-only pay structure guarantees a previously agreed upon amount of money, paid each year. This type of compensation has lower risk because your pay does not depend on sales performance. But it also does not offer much in the way of incentive and can be very limiting. Awards for performance can come only in the form of a renegotiated contract or bonuses. Consistent and substantial bonuses, especially in comparison to your base salary, can create some strange side effects with regard to timing. If the majority of your pay comes in one month, then you must be able to divvy your pay out over the other 11 months.

- 24k base
-

71

SALARY WITH COMMISSION

The most basic of commission structures, salary with commission offers an annual base pay supplemented by commission on all sales. The base can come in the form of a salary or a set hourly rate, with a guaranteed set of workable hours. It offers incentive for performance while limiting some risk associated with commission, because of the base salary. However, it's possible your commission percentage will be lower than other commission-based pay structures because your employer is stomaching some of the risk.

COMMISSION ONLY

The commission-only pay structure offers a percentage of each sale made. While it offers the most incentive of any pay structure, you must be able to close sales efficiently or you will not be paid. Number of hours worked is also not considered, increasing the importance of your ability to close sales. This is the riskiest of compensation structures for the employee, but it also can offer the most rewards. There are multiple variations of the commission-only pay structure.

> ▶ **Variable.** This is the same in concept as a regular commission-only structure, with the difference being that your commission rate will fluctuate, depending on whether you meet or exceed sales goals and by how much. This variability increases both earning potential and uncertainty. Moving commission scales can cause salespeople to run hard at the end of quarters and create an unnecessary feel of seasonality.

retainer w/commission (salary)

▶ **Draw against commission.** In this structure, you're given a predetermined advance on your commission at the beginning of the pay period. This provides money to operate your personal finances from the start, but the advanced pay will be subtracted or drawn from your commission at the end of the pay period. If you don't earn commission up to the draw during the period, then you will owe your employer the difference. Your deficit can usually be paid back later during a more profitable period, but be careful. If you have multiple underachieving periods, your debt to your employer can escalate quickly.

▶ **Residual commission.** Success on a residual commission structure will depend on sustaining long-term relationships with your customers. After gaining an account, you will earn commission on it as long as it generates revenue for the company. A growing sales base and referrals can quickly increase income under this structure. However, losing an account can have a big impact on your overall income, proving the importance of maintaining those long-term relationships. Residual income—or *renewal income*, as it's often called—is often paired with first-year commissions. This is a common compensation structure in both the insurance and financial industries.

All of these different compensation structures can create unnecessary confusion and complication. *The Commissioner* salary process will bring clarity and ease to your financial life.

All of the money you earn from your employer, no matter the form, will flow into your Commissioner pool. From that pool, your new salary will be created.

Depending on your compensation plan, your base salary may disappear. A weaning must take place. A disappearing salary is indicative of a 100 percent commission being on the horizon. You cannot wait until your 100 percent commission structure is here before you decide to start caring about managing your commission income.

FLIPPING THE SCRIPT ON VARIABLE INCOME

One strange effect of having a variable income is that you begin to measure your life's satisfaction on an income performance scale. Good months begin to equal a good life, and bad months begin to equal the opposite of a good life. Our attention is drawn to our bad months because our bad months cause the most stress. But a lack of money isn't the issue.

Remove income from the equation for a moment. From a career perspective, you *should* scrutinize your bad months. Our bad months can define our career in a not-so-hot way. What skills are broken? What processes need to be tweaked? Figure these things out, and your bad months become okay months. And then your okay months become good months. And so on and so forth.

Now, remove your income from great months. What happens next? Nothing. Nothing at all. Either you can keep having great months or you can regress back to good months. But unless you make a point to remove your income from your great months, you'll be in trouble. It's the money, in your great months, that's a massive part of the problem.

You know the drill. Have a huge month: relax. The satisfaction, accolades, and money that come with a big month often cause us to exhale. There's nothing wrong with blowing off some steam and bleeding some air from the pressure-release valve. But your big months are supposed to be your springboard into something better—not something better this month, but better for a long time. Your big months need to bring stability, not pleasure.

I'm asking you to stop linking big months to any sort of consumer gratification. In fact, I'm asking you to have a huge month and then buckle down like you've never buckled down in your life. I want you to push yourself to spend *less* money in your good months. Simply by buckling down during your good months, you can turn a good month into a great month.

Think about this for a second. There are two ways to create a surplus: You can either make more money than you spend or spend less than you're going to make. I realize those two processes seem like the same idea, but they aren't. If you're able to create a surplus in a given month due to increased income, you can create an even larger surplus with an even bigger impact by reducing spending in that month. It's time to smooth out the bumps. It's time to pay yourself a salary.

YOUR SALARY

The key to financial success is budgeting. No one wants to hear this. No one wants to admit this. And most people don't even want to consider this. Budgeting well is nearly impossible when you have a variable income. It's not a matter of hitting a moving target. Your expenses are the target, and they aren't really moving. Instead, your arrows are moving. A variable income messes with your arrows. Your job is to steady your arrows and create a consistent quantity and quality of ammunition.

You established a budget in Chapter 3; now you are going to determine a salary and then pay yourself that salary indefinitely. Your new monthly salary is going to be based off of your monthly salary need. Your monthly salary need is calculated by subtracting other household income not linked to your commission income from your monthly household expenses. Other sources of income will include things like your significant other's income, rental income, investment income, and/or any other regular income stream. If this other income is reliable, renewable, and regular, then use it to offset your monthly household expenses. The remaining income need becomes your new salary. If you don't have any additional income coming into your household, then your new salary will equal your monthly expenses.

For example, if your significant other nets $2,000 per month and your monthly household expenses are $4,500, then your new salary will be $2,500 net per month.

Or, if your household expenses are $4,000 per month, and you don't have any additional household income, then your new salary is $4,000 net per month.

THE POOL

All of the revenue related to your commission or variable-income job goes into the Commissioner pool. From that pool, you will pay yourself your salary. It's highly unlikely that each payment you receive from your employer will be exactly your new salary amount. If it were, you wouldn't really have a variable income. The pay from your employer will be either higher or lower than your salary amount. If the pay from your employer is higher, that particular pay will create a surplus in your Commissioner pool. If the pay from your employer is lower, you will need to draw the difference from your Commissioner pool.

Your Commissioner pool allows surplus months to accumulate, and the pool will allow you to access money during lower-paying months. Use the following table to keep track of the revenue from your employer, your salary, the pay period surplus/shortage, and your running pool total. Ideally, you should be able to use the monthly pool, meaning you create your salary using monthly numbers. But I know better than that. It's tough to take a weekly variable income and create a monthly fixed salary out of it. Therefore, I've provided an example of how the pool works, as well as pools for monthly and weekly pay frequency. Use the pool that reflects the frequency with which your employer pays you.

Your pool is everything. However, it is not your emergency fund. This is where confusion can set in. Your pool is designed to protect your income; your emergency fund is designed to protect your pool. If you need new tires, you need to take your pet to the vet, or you need to buy a gift for grandma, don't take

Month	Revenue from Your Employer	Your New Salary	Surplus/ Shortage	Running Pool Total
Month 1	$4,000	$3,000	$1,000	$1,000
Month 2	$5,000	$3,000	$2,000	$3,000
Month 3	$2,000	$3,000	-$1,000	$2,000
Month 4	$1,000	$3,000	-$2,000	0
Month 5	$3,000	$3,000	0	0
Month 6	$4,000	$3,000	$1,000	$1,000
Month 7	$4,000	$3,000	$1,000	$2,000
Month 8	$5,000	$3,000	$2,000	$4,000
Month 9	$4,000	$3,000	$1,000	$5,000
Month 10	$3,000	$3,000	0	$5,000
Month 11	$4,000	$3,000	$1,000	$6,000
Month 12	$2,000	$3,000	-$1,000	$5,000

Month	Revenue from Your Employer	Your New Salary	Surplus/ Shortage	Running Pool Total
Month 1				
Month 2				
Month 3				
Month 4				
Month 5				
Month 6				
Month 7				
Month 8				
Month 9				
Month 10				
Month 11				
Month 12				

Week	Revenue from Your Employer	Your New Salary	Surplus/ Shortage	Running Pool Total
Week 1				
Week 2				
Week 3				
Week 4				
Week 5				
Week 6				
Week 7				
Week 8				
Week 9				
Week 10				
Week 11				
Week 12				
Week 13				

it from your Commissioner pool. Your Commissioner pool should not be used for anything other than paying yourself a salary.

When life's little emergencies arise, you will use your emergency fund to handle them. You will build your emergency fund by listing it as a budget line item. In fact, that's what the 10 percent savings category is for. Again, do not use your Commissioner pool as some sort of glorified slush fund. You will undo all of your diligence and hard work.

WHAT IFS

Upon completing your household budget and determining your salary need by subtracting other household income from your monthly budget needs, you may find that your salary income need is higher than the paychecks you typically receive from your employer. This is a problem. Not only is it a problem, but it's also a problem that requires significant action. When your newly established salary need is higher than the revenue available through your job, you have two options: reduce your monthly budget needs or make more money. You have no other option.

The wisest thing to do is to reduce your monthly budget needs, even if you have to do this temporarily. If your work income is consistently less than your bills, then your problem isn't the structure of your pay. People waste a tremendous amount of time blaming their pay structure for their financial problems, but a regular budget shortage isn't the problem of your pay structure. A regular budget shortage is often the result of committing yourself to too many monthly obligations. Maybe your cable bill is too high. Maybe you bought too much house or car. Or maybe your food budget is out of control. Whatever your particular reality is, it must change.

Do everything in your power to give yourself a fighting chance. Clean house. No, don't hire a housecleaner. Clear out your financial obligations. Go out to eat less. Cancel your cable for a few months. Or take more drastic steps like changing up your housing situation. A budgeted shortage will not fix itself.

Your other option is to earn more income. I know; that's what you've been trying to do! But if you continue to operate at a significant budget deficit, you need to try something drastically different. Either get an additional gig to supplement your income or change primary jobs. I don't want you to give up on a variable-income job because you are struggling financially, but I also don't want you to bang your head against the wall for months on end.

A part-time job may do the trick. There's nothing wrong with having multiple jobs. Quite the opposite, in fact. There's little more noble than having multiple jobs when that's what the situation calls for. Your additional job can stabilize your financial life until your variable-income gig begins to at least meet your monthly budget needs. If you can objectively say the income from your primary gig will be on the rise soon, then buckle down and hang on tight. If there isn't any light at the end of the income tunnel, then you must make a difficult decision. That decision might just be to move on. ✓ 12 months

Before you make the decision to change jobs, make sure you have exhausted all opportunities to reduce your monthly budget needs. In most cases, leaving your current job is an irreversible decision. Be sure it's the only option left.

YOUR SALARY WILL BRING STABILITY

The very first goal with regard to this process is to create financial stability. Once you get in the groove, you'll notice that your financial stress will start to subside, and you can focus more on being good at your job, and not worrying about making ends meet. While stability is the first step, it isn't even close to the last step. Next up on the agenda is to eventually give yourself a raise, pay yourself a raise, and oh yes, build wealth.

CHAPTER 5

RAISES AND BONUSES

You didn't get into commission sales or a career with a variable income so that you could achieve a moderate income. That's not to suggest that you accepted this sort of compensation system solely based on high-income potential. But the eat-what-you-kill model suggests that you can eat whatever you kill, no matter how much you kill. Your employer may have a bonus structure that rewards you for exceptional performance, as they should. And the really good news is that you can reward yourself for a solid performance as well. When you manage your finances using *The Commissioner* model, you get to pay yourself bonuses, too.

There are some ground rules you should familiarize yourself with. For instance, the bonus your employer may pay you still needs to flow through your Commissioner pool. Why should it, you ask? My answer is, why shouldn't it? Theoretically, celebrating bonuses when you haven't really even stabilized your pay is a great way to have a rubber-band financial life. And no, I don't mean a rubber band around a wad of hundred-dollar bills. Constantly stretching and shrinking your financial life around your money isn't fun. I don't care if your revenue is commission, base salary, performance bonus, holiday bonus, or part of a ransom; all money needs to flow through your pool.

You see, when we start calling money different things, such as base income, commission, and bonus, then we start assigning different jobs to the money—many times when we shouldn't. You have to stop doing that. There is a chance that you're able to separate your income sources and assign particular jobs to each stream, but you would be in the minority. If all the money that comes in flows through the pool, thus normalizing all income sources, you'll be able to avoid some of the dangerous emotions that accompany seemingly alternate proceeds.

Commission sales is a relatively emotional career choice. There are highs and lows. It's hard to think of too many scenarios that leave you feeling better than landing a big account or closing a huge sale. And on the flipside, a slump is the worst. What I'm suggesting is that you separate the career and mental highs and lows from the financial highs and lows. Your job is hard enough without every sale dictating your chance at financial success.

Now that you're on a salary, which was determined by your true financial needs, a true income increase is eventually both warranted and necessary. You have two choices:

▶ Give yourself a raise.

▶ Pay yourself a bonus.

You must understand that giving yourself a raise and paying yourself a bonus aren't the same. In fact, the two couldn't be any more different. And while there are advantages and disadvantages to both moves, your personality and your propensity to succumb to the ills of human nature will truly determine which path you choose.

THE COMMISSIONER INCOME RAISE

If you don't give yourself a raise, you'll go crazy. While there are several benefits and moments of glory to using *The Commissioner* system, giving yourself a raise is among the greatest. You can justify giving yourself a raise for a few different reasons:

▶ Your pool is growing at a ridiculous pace. If you are exceeding your salary payment month after month, then consider increasing your salary. Upon choosing to do this, you still must remain cognizant of your financial priorities and budgeting efficiency. Giving yourself a raise because you can and then wasting the raise on solely expanding your lifestyle is regrettable in both the short and the long term. In the short term, you will create a dependency on this higher of level of income, which destroys the flexibility of a lean budget. The long-term damage is much more serious and much more permanent. You will have missed the opportunity to grow your net worth, which injures your quest for financial independence.

Proceed cautiously unless your pool has grown to four times your monthly salary. Start with a 10 percent raise and give yourself three months to see how it fits. If it's all good and you have no ill effects, try another 10 percent raise.

▶ You receive a bonus from your employer in excess of three months' salary. No matter the frequency of your employer's bonus payments, a bonus in excess of three months' income can justify raising your salary. Of course, it would be foolish to increase your salary to the level of the bonus, because that move could prove to be unsustainable.

A raise of up to 20 percent may be warranted if your revenue is consistently above your average salary. A $5,000 salary can become a $6,000 salary when a bonus from your employer in excess of $15,000 is deposited into your Commissioner pool.

▶ Your pool reaches four times your monthly salary via regular pool deposits. Great job, you've created stability. Give yourself a raise. If seasonality isn't an issue for you, and your revenue success appears to be sustainable, you can justify giving yourself a raise in the 33 percent range. For instance, if your salary is $5,000 and your pool swells to $20,000, you can increase your salary to $6,650.

Don't lose your head. Your salary increases should not create any new immediate obligations. Use the raise to build wealth and secure your future. Don't use your raise to make your financial life more complicated.

THE COMMISSIONER BONUS

A bonus can provide your financial life with an instant boost. You can completely vanquish a debt, fill an emergency fund, invest money for the long term, or fund a home-improvement project. And sure, I'm sure you can probably go on vacation, too. The reality is, once you've wiped out your debt and funded your emergency fund, you can do whatever in the world you want with a well-earned bonus.

PAYING A BONUS VERSUS INCREASING YOUR INCOME

Take a moment to consider this question: If you didn't rely on the money, would you rather have a $25,000 raise to what you consider to be your "base salary" or an annual $25,000 year-end bonus? This is a very important question. Taking the $25,000 raise creates some strange risks. If you don't need an additional $25,000 distributed to you throughout the year, why take it? Again, this question is based on the assumption that you don't need the money. What would you do?

If you took the pay increase, don't you take a higher risk in wasting it? I'd argue yes. When it comes to saving and investing money you don't need for monthly expenses, do you think it's harder to save 12 pieces of money (monthly income) or one piece of money (annual bonus)? And if you're thinking "But what if I need the money during the year?" you've got to change your thinking.

Before you give yourself a permanent raise, you need to be able to objectively look at your future revenue prospects. Don't mistake the objective look for pessimism. Your scrutiny of your future revenue prospects isn't a confidence killer. A good example of this would be if a realtor were to see a major housing market downturn on the horizon. If so, a bonus may be more appropriate than creating a situation in which a raise could create future problems.

Once your Commissioner pool exceeds three months' worth of expenses and seasonality isn't an issue, you can pay yourself a bonus. If the months ahead look consistent, pay yourself a bonus equal to the excess over three months' income in your Commissioner pool. For instance, if your salary is $5,000 per month and your pool swells to $20,000, you could pay yourself a bonus of $5,000, because three months' worth of salary is $15,000, and you have $5,000 in excess of that in your pool.

WHAT TO DO WITH A BONUS

Upon receiving "extra" money—whether it's a bonus, overtime pay, a tax-refund check, or a monetary gift—you should turn first to liquidating debt. Recapture your income by paying off the debts that hold your income hostage. If your windfall can wipe out all of your debt, do it. Just make sure you use the future positive cash flow to quickly create a savings.

If you can't wipe out your debts with your windfall, then make sure you set at least $500 aside in an emergency fund. If you already have $1,000 or so in savings, then use the whole windfall for debt liquidation. Pay off your debts in order from smallest balance to largest balance.

If you don't have any debts, then the windfall becomes a bit more fun. You should strongly consider fully funding your emergency fund with three months' worth of expenses. Once the emergency fund is funded, then you can use future income—regular or windfall—for fun or long-term financial goals. I've seen way too many people waste windfalls. Are my solutions to this problem boring? Arguably, but my solutions prevent a bevy of financial headaches every time the extra-money bell rings.

THE INVISIBLE RAISE

If you have another source of income in your household, such as a significant other's income or rent, then if that income source increases, opportunity is nigh. If your alternate income source increases, then some pressure immediately subsides from your commission-income requirement. And if your household, consisting of a significant other or otherwise, is a lock-step team, then more of your income can flow directly to your financial priorities. Because if the fixed income increases, then your variable income, which was transformed into yet another fixed income via your Commissioner salary, becomes incredibly powerful. I call this the invisible raise. You personally did nothing different, yet your monthly cash flow improved.

If this invisible raise causes you to exhale in relief, you wouldn't be alone. By its nature, a raise is an increase in income not necessarily associated with increased work. Obviously, sometimes a raise is the result of expanding duties and increasing responsibility, but many times a raise is simply a pay raise based on passed time and longevity.

THE DANGERS OF BONUSES AND RAISES

If your journey toward financial wellness is new and you haven't exactly dropped some of your old tendencies and habits, then a raise or bonus could be a giant waste of money. Think of it this way: If you've stopped smoking yet you keep a pack of cigarettes in your glove box, you haven't really quit smoking. There's a delicate balance between trusting yourself and not having faith in your ability to make change stick.

CHAPTER 6

THRIVING AND SURVIVING MONTHS

From time to time, the revenue from your variable-income job will be less than the salary you pay yourself. Technically, this is called a *shortage*. A shortage isn't the end of the world, and your Commissioner pool should easily absorb it, especially if it's a moderate shortage. But what if it's a major shortage? A major shortage can be an anomaly or a major problem. For the purpose of *The Commissioner*, we'll call this a surviving month. An occasional surviving month is okay, but frequent surviving months could signal a much bigger problem. To make sure your surviving months aren't the result of a bigger problem, take yourself through the following checklist:

Surviving-month checklist:

▶ How is next month looking?

▶ How many surviving months have you had in a row?

▶ How much money is left in your Commissioner pool?

▶ Are you concerned with your immediate financial future?

If the surviving-month checklist doesn't raise any additional red flags, then your Commissioner pool will do its job, just like it's supposed to do. If the surviving-month checklist has illuminated some deeper issues, unfortunately your Commissioner pool will act only as a Band-Aid.

When facing a bigger financial problem, keep your head. Exhaust your cost-cutting measures and explore additional income opportunities. Just know that you must take action. You cannot wait out a major financial problem. You cannot ignore it. It will not go away just because you want it to. It will only go away when you level a measured response.

BIG MONEY, BIG PROBLEMS

I used to love thriving months. Now? I don't really care either way. Am I jaded and callous? Not really. I just know that all money, whether it's big, small, or normal, will flow into my Commissioner pool. I didn't always think this way. It's only been since I've adopted a healthy view of thriving months that I've been able to make precisely calculated business and personal finance decisions.

Now, every time I have a thriving month, I run myself through the thriving checklist. You should, too.

Thriving-month checklist:

- ▶ Will your revenue dip back below your average next month?

- ▶ How many thriving months have you had in a row?

- ▶ Is it time for a raise or bonus?

- ▶ Can you leverage this thriving month to create more thriving months?

THE COMMISSIONER SUPER-MOVE

For a moment, let's step away from the world of money and into the world of fitness. Imagine you are focusing on improving your health, which in this case involves weight loss. If you were to have an amazing workout that burned a tremendous number of calories, you have three choices on how you could handle your food intake for the day. You could:

► **Eat more food.** Since your workout created a caloric deficit, you could use this caloric deficit to consume more food than usual, thus bringing the ultimate level of pleasure.

► **Eat the same amount of food.** If you chose to eat the same amount of food on a day in which you burned a tremendous number of calories, then you'll almost certainly lock in a certain level of weight loss. In fact, this is one of the principles behind weight loss: You consume fewer calories than you burn. And when you burn a ton of calories on a good workout day, then your normal (healthy) food choices can lead to weight loss.

► **Eat less.** If you really want to guarantee that your amazing workout pays off, then magnify its effect on your health by safely reducing your caloric intake for the day. When you do this, the caloric deficit grows even higher.

You can accomplish the same idea on a variable income. If you are looking for a lifetime of financial success, then employ the Commissioner Super-Move. Your choices when faced with a thriving month are to:

► **Spend more money.** Because your increased income created a surplus, you could use this surplus to spend more money, thus bringing the ultimate level of pleasure.

▶ **Spend the same amount of money.** If you chose to spend the same amount of money in a month in which you earned a great deal of money, then you almost certainly will lock in a net-worth increase. In fact, this is one of the principles behind budgeting: Spend less than you earn.

▶ **Spend less money.** If you really want to guarantee that your thriving month pays off, then magnify its effect on your financial life by safely reducing your spending during the thriving month. When you do this, the surplus grows even higher.

What's odd is that thriving months are more difficult to deal with than surviving months. It's hard to make spending mistakes when you don't have much money coming in. It's much easier to make spending mistakes when money is abundant. Let me explain by using my favorite resource, toilet paper, as an example. As unpleasant as it is to think about, we've all been faced with the very alarming prospect of being stranded without the appropriate amount of toilet paper. It may sound humorous now, but it's extremely unfunny in the moment. The point is, when faced with cardboard, you will survive in any way possible, and you'll learn two lessons because of it:

▶ Check the supply levels before you use the bathroom!

▶ Be resourceful.

It's easy to be wasteful when you have a full roll and to forget what you went through when faced with an empty one.

If you want, you can chalk it up to the more money = more problems idea. The dangers of a thriving month are especially troublesome if your definition of success itself is subpar. Should you feel successful simply because your revenue was high in a particular month? Not exactly.

Take a moment and ask yourself what financial success looks like. Does it mean that you have the perfect job? Does it mean that you make $300k per year? Let's define success for you and then make sure that it makes sense. Let's ensure that your definition won't actually lead you to a financial catastrophe. I think through my own journey of "success" discovery, and I shake my head in awe. I almost screwed up badly.

Over the last 12 years, I have defined my own idea of personal success in two polar-opposite ways.

My early definition of success was to be able to afford whatever I wanted. Okay, that's not terrible, but it's not great. This definition had me chasing dollars to accomplish my goal. I have found that to be a fruitless journey. Being able to afford whatever I want doesn't really work because my idea of "afford" is pretty subjective. Most people get into financial trouble because they buy things that they subjectively think they can afford, when in fact they objectively cannot.

My current definition of success has me feeling very peaceful. To me, success is not striving to have more, but constantly needing less to feel satisfied with my life. I don't want to strive to have more; I want to strive to be comfortable with less. Since I have taken on this definition, my income and wealth have grown substantially. I believe our wealth grows when we don't focus on wealth. Instead, as you are about to learn, wealth comes when you properly juggle time, money, and resourcefulness.

CHAPTER 7
WEALTH

I've found that people tend to overcomplicate their quest for wealth in several ways.

If your income consistently rises and you don't consistently save your raises after you achieve a certain level of comfort, then you are creating a nearly insurmountable mountain of dependency. You can accumulate a million dollars, but if you need $100,000 per year in retirement, then you're going to be in trouble. If you focus on the wealth, then you are focusing on the wrong goal. People act differently when wealth, not resourcefulness, is the goal. Greed and emotions can cloud otherwise good judgment.

Think about most of the financial planning commercials you've seen. What is the message? In my unabashed opinion, the message is that accumulation is the key. I disagree with this message. You can't accumulate money without resourcefulness. And as you've learned in *The Commissioner*, resourcefulness creates stability, too. When wealth is the goal, then the focus turns to assets, not income. This means that people worry more about what their investment choices are than how their income should fund their investments.

Maybe I'm crazy, but dangling wealth in front of people to get them to care doesn't seem sincere to me. It's a discredit to humanity when you make financial wellness about wealth. In most cases, I believe that behavior is to blame for both success and failure. That's why I want the discussion to revolve around the behaviors that lead to resourcefulness.

When wealth is the goal, you will *always* measure satisfaction on a monetary scale. But I don't believe we sell ourselves short when we strive to be resourceful.

Resourcefulness isn't about being cheap. It's not about penny-pinching. To me, it all boils down to this very simple idea: A person who isn't resourceful never has enough resources. Wealth can't be the goal.

SAVINGS VERSUS INVESTING

To begin, there is a gigantic difference between saving and investing. You need to know how to do both. Each requires specific skills and rudimentary habits. And while the terms *saving* and *investing* are often used interchangeably, they shouldn't be.

The purpose of saving is threefold. First, saving allows you to handle short-term, unexpected expenses. We sometimes call these types of things *emergencies*, but they aren't always emergencies. Vacations, home furnishings, and car purchases made with cash aren't emergencies, yet they should be funded with savings, not investments.

The second purpose for savings is to preserve money without taking risks. Although it may seem counterintuitive, you shouldn't be overly concerned with the rate of return you are receiving on your savings account. Saving itself isn't concerned with growth; it's concerned with preservation. Although some investments may find themselves allocated toward preservation-type goals, investments are usually earmarked for appreciation or income-production. But when investing gets involved in the conversation, the word *risk* arrives with it. Savings generally maintains an absence of risk.

The last purpose of saving is also the most important. By saving a portion of your current income now, you are declaring your independence from your total income. The more money you save on a monthly basis, the less likely you are to develop dependence on that portion of your income. If you want to avoid living paycheck to paycheck, in the negative sense, your spending must remain independent of your increasing income throughout your career. Otherwise, no matter how much you earn, you'll find a way to spend it.

You need to understand how different types of investments work. You need to know how they are different and which ones are right for you. While a financial advisor would certainly be able to assist you with this, it's in your best interest to have a better than cursory understanding of the investment world.

Regardless of whether you are saving money or investing money, you are increasing your net worth.

THE ROLE OF NET WORTH AS A WEALTH-BUILDING TOOL

Net worth is the greatest metric in all of the financial world. It's a powerful, misunderstood tool that can drive wealth higher, and better yet, pull desperate people out of the doldrums of debt.

Why is net worth such a great measure? Simply put, it measures various financial activities in a very complex way. If you monitor your net worth, you will be able to see the impact of making debt payments, saving money, and investing money, and you can even watch your investments' market performance or simple appreciation. You can obtain your net worth by subtracting your current debts from your current assets. As you know, assets are things such as real estate, savings, and investments. And debts are...debts.

Let's take a look at a couple of different examples to help you better understand this. First up, let's examine the financial life of 36-year-old marketing consultant Jacob.

January 1, 2014

Assets:	**$285,000**
House:	$240,000
401(k):	$35,000
Savings:	$10,000
Debts:	**$190,000**
Mortgage:	$190,000
Net worth:	**$95,000**

As you can clearly see, Jacob's net worth is $95,000. If Jacob takes care of business and makes some prudent financial decisions, then he can make some shockingly good financial progress. For instance, over the next year, if Jacob pays his mortgage (12 months of principal payments for a total of $9,000 toward his principal), puts money into his 401(k) ($8,000 deferred from his paycheck and $2,500 matched from his employer), and saves into his savings account ($200 per month), then his net worth will increase by $21,900 by the end of the year. And that doesn't even include the possible market appreciation of his home and/or return on his 401(k). By measuring his net worth, Jacob learns that he can move the financial needle by

$21,900, or 23 percent of his net worth, at the beginning of the year.

Let's now examine the financial life of 33-year-old school counselor Jen.

January 1, 2014

Assets:	**$750**
Savings:	$750
Debts:	**$25,000**
Medical bills:	$7,500
Credit cards:	$17,500
Net worth:	**−$24,250**

Jen isn't feeling too great about her financial state. Jen never looks at her debts. They stress her out. "What's the point?" she often asks herself. But then Jen decides to measure her activity for one year. She works hard to pay down her credit cards by $6,500. And she pays down $3,500 on her medical bills. Additionally, she starts contributing to her school's 403(b), up to the match. Thus, she deposits $1,200, and the school matches $1,200. On December 31, Jen does the math and realizes that she increased her net worth by $12,400, or a 51.1 percent increase. Sure, Jen now has a net worth of −$11,850, but she's made *amazing* progress. And better yet, she's enthused. She's been working really hard on making financial changes, but she always felt like she was running in place. But she clearly isn't running in place: She improved her situation by more than 50 percent. That's phenomenal!

Can you imagine eating well, exercising regularly, feeling sad about your fitness progress, yet never weighing yourself to see whether you are getting any results? Yeah, it happens all the time—in exercise and in finance. When you don't measure your net worth, you miss the opportunity to reward your progress and hard work. Paying down debt can feel mundane, but it isn't. In fact, if you pay down $10,000 worth of debt, it has the same effect on your net worth as if you saved $10,000. In both cases, it's a net worth increase of $10,000.

Do you want to start viewing your debt pay-down process differently? Then start measuring your net worth. The only debt I personally have is my mortgage, but I love figuring my net worth so I can measure the impact of my mortgage principal payments. I sincerely celebrate each mortgage payment, and so should you. The possibilities are endless when net worth is your go-to metric. Take for instance the story of pharmaceutical rep Brent.

Brent had lots of money. He was *consumed* with monitoring his portfolio's performance on a daily basis. Like many people, Brent lost sight of reality. He was so concerned with how well his broker was doing that he neglected to put any more of his income toward his investment portfolio. Instead, he chose to spend wildly because he had an $80,000 portfolio—even though, frankly, his portfolio was struggling. He lost 10 percent, or $8,000, in one year. The crazy thing is that Brent was completely wasting $1,500 per month on really stupid stuff. If Brent had monitored and utilized the net worth metric correctly, he would have increased his contributions to his portfolio by $18,000, despite his $8,000 loss. Not only would his net worth have increased, but he also would have hypothetically purchased more investments at a lower price, thus ensuring more profit once the portfolio turned around.

I love using net worth because it can reinvigorate individuals who've already amassed great wealth yet have fallen on apathetic times. It can refresh individuals who've dug themselves such a deep hole that they can't muster the fortitude to glance at their actual debt levels. I love using net worth to show anyone and everyone that purposeful financial decision-making will always lead to progress. As I said, net worth is the greatest financial metric in all of the financial world.

In practice, paying your debts is relatively simple compared to figuring out where your savings and investments should go.

TYPES OF INVESTMENTS AND INVESTMENT VEHICLES

You may not aspire to be a brilliant investor, but you should aspire to understand investing. It's imperative that you understand certain terms and jargon of the financial industry. Every day of my life, I encounter people in their fifties and sixties who have no idea of the difference between a mutual fund and a stock. There is a difference, by the way, and it matters.

I don't know your current financial aptitude, so we'll start on the base level and work our way up to slightly more complicated concepts. If you understand the following terms, you'll be in good shape.

STOCK

A stock is a share of the value of a company that can be purchased, sold, or traded as an investment. Although there are two main types of stocks—preferred stock and common stock—you're likely to be exposed only to common stock.

As an owner of preferred stock, you'll be among the first to receive dividends when the company either distributes extra cash during good times or liquidates assets during times of trouble. In addition, your dividend payout will be more consistent and predictable, as preferred stockholders are paid at regular intervals.

The same does not apply to common stockholders. As an owner of common stock, you'll receive payouts only when the company's board of directors approves a payout. You'll also be the last to receive dividends during liquidation, as companies must pay all preferred stockholders before they pay common stockholders.

Some stocks pay you, as a partial owner of the company, a portion of the profits. This disbursement is called a *dividend*. The dividend may be 30 to 40 cents per share, or it may be up to $3 or $4. You can reinvest these dividends into more shares of stock through things like Dividend Reinvestment Programs (DRIPs).

All in all, when you own stock in a company, you own a piece of the company—albeit a small piece.

BOND

A bond is an investment in which you serve as the lender—to a company, to a bank, or to the government. They borrow your money and promise to pay you back in full, with interest payments.

The more respectable the institution—such as the U.S. government or a large-scale corporation with a track record of long-term success—the safer the investment. With safer investments come lower interest rates and lower payouts. The riskier the loan, the more interest is up for grabs. You've probably heard the term *junk bond*. It refers to a bond that isn't rated very highly, yet pays a pretty handsome amount of interest. The risk for default (the bond being worth nothing) is higher, but the returns can be great, too. This fact alone can dispel the myth that bonds are collectively safe.

In addition, the duration of the bond plays into how lucrative it might be for you—the longer the duration of the bond period, the higher the payout.

In the end, when you buy a bond, you let an institution borrow your money.

MUTUAL FUND

A mutual fund is a collection of stocks and bonds managed by professional investors who diversify investments across a wide range of industries in an attempt to minimize risk. A mutual fund might contain investments in technology, agriculture, and pharmaceutical companies or any other industry, all in an attempt to ensure that the gains in one industry offset the losses in another.

Mutual funds earn income for you through the dividends on the stocks included in the fund and through interest from the bonds. If your stocks or bonds increase in price over the course of the year and your fund manager sells them at a higher price, the fund will experience a capital gain, the profits of which will be shared with investors.

EXCHANGE TRADED FUND

I should probably start by defining *index*. An index is a selection of stocks that is used to gauge the health and performance of the overall stock market. Whenever you hear or read "the market was up 38 points today," what they are talking about is the index. For instance, the Standard & Poor's 500 (S&P 500) Index is a group of 500 stocks that is used to measure the tone and direction of the stock market in general.

Exchange Traded Funds (ETFs) track the yields and returns of a specific index, such as the S&P 500 or the Dow Jones. Unlike other index funds, which try to beat the average performance of their index, an ETF attempts to mirror its index performance. In other words, if your Dow Jones ETF is performing exactly like the Dow Jones, it's doing well.

ETFs offer many of the same benefits of mutual funds—they're professionally managed and created to minimize risk—but the similarities end there. ETFs can be traded like a stock continually throughout the trading day, whereas mutual funds are priced only after the market closes. And because ETFs don't attempt to beat the market, they're less maintenance for managers, resulting in lower management fees.

As a result of these advantages, ETFs have become increasingly popular over the course of the last decade.

INDEX FUND

Index funds are similar to ETFs in that their success is tied to how well they replicate their index performance. For example, an index fund tracking the Dow Jones Industrial Average would own all of the same stocks as the Dow Jones.

Because index funds require minimal maintenance, they are passively managed. As a result, they have lower expense ratios (0.2 percent to 0.5 percent on average) than actively managed funds (which usually fall somewhere between 1.3 percent and 2.5 percent).

Index funds have grown in popularity both because of lower expense ratios and because market watchers realized that the indexes were outperforming mutual funds over the long term.

TARGET-DATE FUNDS

Target-date funds are investments that link investment selections with distance from retirement. Each target-date fund is linked to a particular year—theoretically, the year you wish to retire. Once you invest in this target-date fund, your investment allocation flows along what is called a *glide path*. This glide path consistently shifts the percentages of stock, bonds, and cash over time until they are at the "ideal" percentages to ready you for retirement. To add some additional complexity, a few target-date funds are meant to usher you through retirement, not just to retirement. The remainder of the target-date funds simply prepares your portfolio for retirement, but isn't necessarily appropriate to hold when you are retired.

I've always thought of our investment allocations as cake recipes. Add the right amount of stock, the right amount of bonds, and the right amount of cash, and you will have a money-cake cooked to your liking. Target-date funds are prepackaged cakes. The ingredients are all right there, the cake is baked, and you can't adjust the recipe. Strangely, people mess this part up. If you have a target-date fund in your portfolio, along with other funds, then you are basically pouring flour and/or sugar on the top of a pre-baked cake that you just emptied into a mixing bowl from a plastic wrapper. Yeah, that's not going to taste good. When you combine a target-date fund with other investments within your account, you may create unintended consequences. Target-date funds were designed to be the only investment in your account.

If I were forced to rank investing strategies within a retirement plan, target-date funds would find themselves in third place. In first place, you'd find a relationship with an investment advisor who can help you make the right investment selections according to both your risk tolerance and your time horizon. Second place belongs to educating yourself and managing your investments in a suitable, unemotional way. Realistically, educating yourself and managing your investments in a suitable, unemotional way is intensely challenging. Sound investment strategy isn't built on guts and panache; it's built on discipline and patience. And while doing it yourself is the second-best option, it's the worst option if you objectively don't know what you're doing.

Which brings us to third place. Target-date funds are perfect for individuals who don't have an investment advisor and don't take the time to thoroughly educate themselves on the principles of investing. Target-date funds generally have slightly higher fees than a la carte investments, but there's an obvious reason for that. They're alive! The investment allocations shift the closer you get to your target retirement date, and you don't have to do anything.

IRA

One of the more popular ways to save for retirement is through an Individual Retirement Account (IRA), also called a traditional IRA. You can put almost any type of investment inside an IRA, including stocks, bonds, mutual funds, ETFs, and/or index funds. Depending on your income, contributions to an IRA may be deductible on your income-tax filing. They essentially have the same tax status as a 401(k). Additionally, an IRA allows your investments to grow without being subjected to capital gains or dividend income taxes. However, when you receive IRA distributions during retirement, your distributions will be considered income and will be subject to income tax.

An IRA is a popular choice for people who aren't offered an employer-sponsored retirement plan, such as a 401(k). A Roth IRA is also a popular option.

ROTH IRA

A Roth IRA is similar to a traditional IRA in that it allows you to direct part of your pre-tax income into investments intended to grow over time. However, where the traditional IRA is tax deferred, meaning you don't pay taxes on the investment until it is distributed in retirement, the Roth IRA is taxed up front, and you don't have to pay taxes when you receive funds later.

And by later, I mean once you reach the age of 59-1/2.

401(k)

Most employers offer 401(k) plans as part of their compensation packages. A 401(k) enables you to make a contribution from each paycheck into a tax-deferred plan. Many employers offer a matching program, in which they will match your contribution up to a specified limit. So if the 401(k) match limit is 3 percent and you contribute 3 percent of your salary, your employer will match it, creating a total investment of 6 percent of your salary into your plan.

Needless to say, you should always save at least the maximum amount of your employer match, or you'll be leaving money on the table. And that's never a good thing.

529 COLLEGE SAVINGS PLAN

Qualified tuition programs—or 529s, as most people call them—were created under the Small Business Job Protection Act of 1996. They work a lot like Roth IRAs in terms of taxation, but 529 plans are designed to help you save for a college education. It can be your college education or your child's college education. It doesn't really matter.

Every state has its own 529 College Savings Plan. You can invest your money in any of them. You don't have to go to school or live in the state's plan in which you invest, either. Many people, myself included, choose the 529 plan in the state in which they live because of the state tax benefits. Every state has different ways they incentivize or don't incentivize depositors to save for college. Although fees and investment performance are certainly important factors in making your 529 selection, state tax benefits are hard to pass up. If your state has allowed for tax credits or anything else of the sort in relation to depositing into a 529 College Savings Plan, you should explore it thoroughly before looking to another state's plan.

WHY YOU CAN'T WAIT TO INVEST

What people fail to understand is that when you don't save for the future, you can't use time as a tool. When your money grows, it (ideally) grows every year. For instance, if you invest $5,000 that earns 8 percent, then after one year you will have $5,400. Great. But if you make this initial investment 20 years from your retirement goal versus five years from your retirement goal, then time makes all the difference.

Take a look at the following table. Let's say you are 30 years old, and you decide to invest $5,000 per year for just five years and leave the money alone for 20 years from the day of the initial investment. And let's assume that you earn an 8 percent rate of return on your money. This is a very reasonable rate of return over a 20-year period. Obviously, you would need to be in some sort of stock-market investment (stocks, ETFs, or mutual funds) to receive that sort of return. At the end of 20 years, you would have $100,493.19. Not too shabby.

Now let's assume you wait to start investing until you are 45 years old. Even if you saved three times the amount of money ($15,000) for five years, you still wouldn't be able to equal the account that started growing at age 30. Money wasn't the issue here; time was the issue.

People tend to think they will have more money to save the older they get. This may or may not be true. Even if it is true, those people will need to save three times the amount if they want to achieve the exact same financial goals. Would you like to invest $25,000 to reach $100,000? Or would you rather invest $75,000?

Time in Years	Investment	Growth	Investment	Growth
1	$5,000.00	$5,400.00		
2	$5,000.00	$11,232.00		
3	$5,000.00	$17,530.56		
4	$5,000.00	$24,333.00		
5	$5,000.00	$31,679.65		
6		$34,214.02		
7		$36,951.14		
8		$39,907.23		
9		$43,099.81		
10		$46,547.79		
11		$50,271.62		
12		$54,293.34		
13		$58.636.81		
14		$63,327.76		
15		$68,393.98		
16		$73,865.50	$15,000.00	$16,200.00
17		$79,774.74	$15,000.00	$33,696.00
18		$86,156.71	$15,000.00	$52,591.68
19		$93,049.25	$15,000.00	$72,999.01
20		$100,493.19	$15,000.00	$95,038.94

Additional complexities appear when you wait to start investing for the future. The closer you are to your time goal of having $100,000 by age 50, the more risk you are forced to take because you need your money to grow unnaturally fast. Conversely, the further you are away from your time goal of having $100,000 by age 50, the less risk you have to take. You could invest less than $5,000 initially at age 30 and still hit your $100,000 goal if you continued investing after the fifth year. Or you could invest $100,000 on your 50th birthday and hit your goal. I'll take option one.

The next time you hear or think that there's plenty of time to invest, check yourself. There's plenty of time for your money to grow, but the longer you wait to invest, the harder it will be.

THREE STEPS TO PREPARE FOR LONG-, MID-, AND SHORT-TERM MONEY NEEDS

To be an effective saver, you need to pay attention to three distinct segments of time: the now, the far off but sooner than you think, and the far off. These three segments are more commonly known as your short-term savings, mid-term savings, and long-term savings. And believe it or not, there is a very specific way you need to build your savings into these different categories.

STEP 1: SET UP YOUR RETIREMENT ACCOUNT, IDEALLY THROUGH YOUR EMPLOYER

You can't, under any circumstances, wait to save for retirement. You must immediately defer a portion of your current income into your retirement savings. For many people, this means a 401(k), 403(b), or 401(a), which you would access through your employer.

Waiting to save for the future is inexcusable for several reasons. First, you probably won't have three streams of retirement income like your parents and grandparents did. A pension, Social Security, and personal investments used to provide a diverse retirement-income strategy. But based on a few policy shifts and planning trends, only 15 percent of the private sector has a defined benefit plan (a pension) today. You're more likely to have two streams of retirement income, Social Security and your own personal savings and investments.

Additionally, if you aren't saving into your company-sponsored retirement plan, you are likely missing out on the employer match. The employer match is when your employer contributes to your retirement plan based on your contributions to your retirement plan. They *match* your contribution up to a predetermined percentage.

If you don't have access to a retirement plan directly through your employer, then you need to set up your own retirement plan. Depending on your situation, you may be eligible for a Roth IRA, Traditional IRA, SIMPLE IRA, SEP IRA, or even a solo 401(k). Your tax advisor will help you understand which plans you are eligible for and will help you determine which plan is best for you. One of the main disadvantages of not having access to an employer-sponsored retirement plan is you won't receive additional "free" compensation in the form of a match.

And while the match is great, unfortunately people have become obsessed with the match. "Pete, I hit the match!" Okay, enough. That's great. You're supposed to hit your match. How much time should I spend celebrating your unwillingness to ignore extra compensation opportunities? Despite what we're led to believe, an employer match isn't an incentive for us to save for retirement, it's a process to weed out people who are terrible at math.

The match is what your employer is willing to contribute to your retirement plan, based on what you contribute to your retirement plan. For instance, if you contribute 3 percent of your annual income to your retirement plan, your employer may match your contribution by also contributing 3 percent to your retirement plan. This is free money. You can try to argue about vesting schedules, illiquidity, or anything else you want, but the reality is if you don't do what it takes to maximize the match, you should barely be considered employable. This is exactly why I want you to stop focusing on the match. I want you to blow it off.

Hitting the match is as elementary as brushing your teeth. Brushing your teeth isn't a goal; you just do it. Hitting the match isn't a goal; you just do it. You are probably wondering what's beyond the match. If I'm asking you to dismiss the importance of the match, then I must be asking you to do something in addition to the match. You are correct. But we need to continue to get weirder for a moment.

"Pete, I put 10 percent of my income into my retirement plan." Okay. Why? "Well, I figure it's a round number, and it just seems to make sense." Yes, it is a round number, and no, it doesn't make sense. Why would a round number make sense? Your retirement plan will be used to replace your income when you retire. What do round numbers have to do with anything? Your goal isn't to live in a world of round numbers and cute rules of thumb. Your goal is to be able to stop working someday.

Ask yourself, what in the world will saving 5 percent or 10 percent of your income do for you come retirement time? In most cases, nothing. It will do nothing. I don't say this to kill your buzz or ruin your day. Your retirement will be different from your parents' and grandparents' retirement based on your number of retirement-income sources. Your retirement will be possible only if you break your dependency on your income and defer tremendous amounts of money into your retirement plan.

You've probably noticed that the term "financial independence" is used often to describe retirement. Financial independence is meant to describe our lack of dependence on work income. But in a very strange twist, most financial-independence (retirement) planning does very little to break income dependency. It really only focuses on accumulating more and more money. Where'd the independence go?

You can create independence by deferring as much money as possible into your retirement plan. In 2014, you could defer $17,500 of your income into your company-sponsored retirement plan (if you were under 50 years old). Your goal is to do that. I'm not kidding. To think your retirement will go well without it is dim. Figure 7.1 shows an example.

If you were to save $17,500 every year, starting today, for 35 years, at an 8 percent rate of return, you'd end up with $3,015,544.

If you were to distribute 4 percent of that money to yourself in retirement (4 percent is widely considered to be the amount of money you should withdraw from your retirement investments

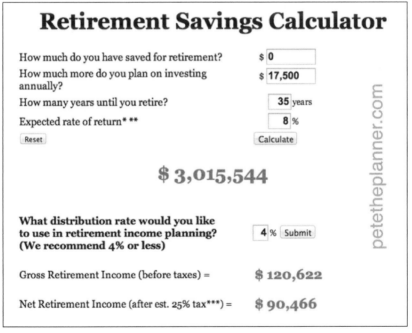

Figure 7.1 Aggressively deferring income.

on an annual basis), you'd receive $120,622 per year gross. Great, huh? Well, you have to pay taxes. Let's estimate a 25 percent effective tax rate. That brings your net income to $90,466. What's that? You're wondering about inflation? Me too. If money loses half of its buying power every 25 years or so, then your $90,466 is going to feel more like $40,000 in today's dollars. Yes, I made lots of assumptions, and contribution limits and tax brackets will change. But the point of this is to give you a general idea of what you're up against. By the way, feel free to use our retirement calculator to run your own scenarios at PeteThePlanner.com/Retirement-Calculator.

What if you contributed $8,000-ish per year? Take a look at Figure 7.2.

Retirement Savings Calculator

How much do you have saved for retirement?	$ 0
How much more do you plan on investing annually?	$ 8,000
How many years until you retire?	35 years
Expected rate of return* **	8 %
Reset	Calculate

$ 1,378,534

What distribution rate would you like to use in retirement income planning? (We recommend 4% or less) — 4 % Submit

Gross Retirement Income (before taxes) = $ 55,141

Net Retirement Income (after est. 25% tax***) = $ 41,356

petetheplanner.com

Figure 7.2 Moderately deferring income.

Looks like your inflation-adjusted retirement income will be less than $20,000 per year. You can't expect to continue your current financial lifestyle, within reason, if you don't put good money away for the future.

The biggest complaint I hear in this regard is "Pete, your retirement savings expectations are unrealistic. Who can afford to save that much?" There's a ton of failed thinking with this complaint. Here's what I know: If you don't save this money, you won't be able to have a reasonable retirement. I know that $3 million and $1.3 million seem like a lot of money, but 35 years from now, it'll be a lot less than you think. Additionally, if you get frisky and distribute your assets at a rate higher than 4 percent, you'll risk running out of money.

The following table is a Monte Carlo simulation from my book, *Mock Retirement*. It's based on a 60 percent stock and 40 percent bond asset mix during retirement. I ran 5,000 simulations, using historical market data, to determine the success rate of your retirement for different distribution rates. If you think an 8 percent chance of failure is no big deal, would you get on a train if the conductor announced prior to leaving the station that the train had an 8 percent chance of crashing? I'd be off that death train faster than you could possibly imagine.

Retirement doesn't feel real for anyone who's 15 years or more from retirement. Because of this, we don't really do the math. And the further out we are from retirement, the more we depend on something mystical to happen to change our financial future. Mystical things don't happen to change our financial paths. Your retirement will work only if you dismiss the glory of your match. Your goal is to max out your retirement plan, not hit some silly match that tricks you into thinking you are doing something about your retirement problem.

60 Percent Stock / 40 Percent Bond

Percent of Portfolio Used per Year	10 Years	15 Years	20 Years	25 Years	30 Years
3.00%	100%	100%	100%	100%	99%
3.50%	100%	100%	100%	98%	96%
4.00%	100%	100%	99%	96%	92%
4.50%	100%	100%	97%	92%	86%
5.00%	100%	100%	94%	85%	79%
5.50%	100%	98%	90%	79%	69%
6.00%	100%	96%	83%	69%	59%
6.50%	100%	92%	75%	60%	48%
7.00%	100%	87%	65%	52%	41%
7.50%	99%	81%	58%	41%	30%
8.00%	98%	74%	47%	32%	23%
8.50%	96%	66%	38%	24%	18%
9.00%	94%	57%	32%	18%	12%

If for some reason your employer doesn't have a company-sponsored retirement plan, then set up an IRA or a Roth IRA on your own. The limits on IRAs and Roth IRAs are much lower than a company-sponsored retirement plan. In 2014, people under the age of 50 were limited to $5,500 per year in contributions, whereas 401(k) contributions could equal $17,500 per year. These contribution limits generally increase over time.

STEP 2: SAVE AT LEAST 10 PERCENT OF YOUR TAKE-HOME PAY INTO A SAVINGS ACCOUNT (EMERGENCY FUND)

Life happens. Whether this means your dog gets sick, your job is eliminated, or you need new tires on your car, at some point in the near future you are going to need money above and beyond your monthly income. I recommend having around $1,000 or so in this savings account while you are battling with consumer debt (such as credit cards). The 10 percent allocation you'd otherwise put toward savings should be used for debt reduction when you have consumer debt. Once it's paid off, you can shift your focus back to saving.

You need to accumulate three months' worth of expenses in your emergency fund. If your monthly expenses are $3,500, then you need $10,500 in your emergency fund. I know what you might be thinking: "That's a lot of money to have earning zero-point-nothing percent in interest." No, it's not. This money is designed to have your back under any circumstance. You can't risk tying it up in illiquid investments or having it decrease in value by investing it in anything other than a savings account or a money market account. If $10,500 seems like a lot of money to you, your goal is to shift your thinking. Your emergency fund will decrease the financial stress in your life, and it will allow you to take additional risks with your midterm bucket of money (which we'll discuss in a moment).

Before we move on, here are a couple of other rules for your emergency fund. It is not down-payment money for a house. It is not new-car money. It is for unexpected expenses. In fact, I'd prefer people use this account for almost any unexpected, involuntary expense. Brakes go out on your car? Use this money. Unexpected medical bill? Use this money. Stop trying to handle unusual expenses with your income. When you try to absorb an unusual expense without tapping into your savings, you end up throwing off your timing. Before you know it, your bills will be due before you get your next paycheck, and you'll wonder what happened. Use your emergency fund and then replenish it with your 10 percent monthly contribution to this savings. Once your short-term bucket is full, your future savings will go somewhere else. The key is that you never break the habit of saving.

STEP 3: CREATE WEALTH BY INVESTING WITH THE MIDTERM BUCKET

I know that I've previously told you I don't like dangling the carrot of you possibly becoming a millionaire, but if it's going to happen, it's because of Step 3. Once you've committed to saving for your retirement (by deferring money into your company-sponsored retirement plan), and once you've secured your present financial life (by saving three months' worth of expenses), then life can get really fun. If you thought spending and acquiring new things was fun, just wait until you get addicted to growth and accumulation.

When you've got more money than you know what to do with, then you need to be throwing this money into the midterm bucket. This midterm bucket is technically called *non-qualified money*—which means it doesn't have any special tax advantage. The money doesn't grow tax deferred, but you don't have to wait until you are 59 1/2 to access the funds in this bucket (as long as you don't put money from this bucket into an annuity). Making regular contributions to this bucket certainly could warrant the need for a financial advisor. Since you've already filled up your emergency fund, you are cranking at least 10 percent (if not more) of your income into this midterm bucket. The investments in this bucket need to fall in line with your risk tolerance, time horizon, and other financial considerations. These complexities are why I would like you to employ a financial advisor at this step in the process.

You're probably wondering what types of investments should go into this bucket. Well, lots of things could go into this bucket—stocks, bonds, mutual funds, ETFs, real estate, or any other investment that doesn't lock up your money until you are 59 1/2 years old. You do need to be aware that some investments in this bucket can create current tax problems for you. Again, talk to a financial advisor or a tax accountant about your particular situation.

And this is where things get really fun. This bucket can be used for anything. It can be used for a down payment on a home, college, a wedding, a vacation, a business, staying home with the kids for a predetermined amount of time, or anything else that tickles your fancy. If you want to enjoy life and not worry about money, then bust your hump to fill your emergency fund so that you can start putting money into this midterm bucket.

Additionally, your goal is to crank up contributions to both the midterm and long-term buckets. Saving your raises helps with this, as does proper budgeting and an overall spirit of financial wellness. And by the way, feel free to take this chapter to your financial advisor and ask them how to best utilize this strategy to build wealth. Under no circumstances should you let your advisor convince you that Step 3 can be skipped in any way, shape, or form.

HIRING A FINANCIAL ADVISOR

Financial advisors are like wine. A higher price point doesn't always equal better results. On top of that, like wine, personal preference and tastes can dictate the consumer's experience and satisfaction. Every person in the world besides you may like a particular wine, but if you don't like it, what's the point of drinking it? You need to understand how your priorities, attitude, and personality intersect with a potential advisor's offerings.

How do you select the right financial advisor? That's a very simple question that elicits stress, fear, and confusion in the average financial consumer. And it's a question that I never fully understood until I stopped working with personal financial planning clients. From the outset, the selection process is overwhelming. Consider the titles alone. How would you even begin to decipher the following jargon?

Financial planner. Investment planner. Investment advisor. Financial consultant. Financial advisor. Registered representative. Financial specialist. Agent. Retirement planner. College planner. Broker.

In the words of my precocious four-year-old, "Good luck with that."

And if you make the right title choice, you'll next need to decide what you want out of an advisor relationship. If you choose to hire a financial advisor, you should expect the person to serve two primary functions. First, your advisor should help you find and evaluate investment opportunities. Second, your advisor should move you forward financially. Your net worth should increase. This means that your debts should decrease and your savings and investments should increase. While these are the reasons to hire a good financial advisor, you'll still need to make sense of who to hire.

You really only need a financial advisor if you are going to invest. It has been my experience that financial advisors offer very little expertise in anything other than investing and technical financial planning. By the way, debt and budgeting generally fall outside this expertise. A good financial advisor will be important to your future. Once you've cleaned up all your debt, budgeting issues, and discipline issues, like we all have to, then follow these tips to pick a great financial advisor.

▶ **Knowledge.** It's weird to even write about this. A great majority of financial industry people have no idea what they are doing. In fact, in 2012 a cat named Orlando outperformed a number of investment advisors in the UK. And no, I don't mean cat as in he was a cool cat. I mean he had whiskers and drank out of a saucer. Orlando threw his toy on a grid filled with different options. Where his toy landed is where the money was invested. The cat dominated the experts who were using traditional means. And by "traditional means," I mean no batting a cat toy across a grid of investments.

No one knows what the market is going to do. No one. They might have a theory as to why it might go up or down, but they don't actually know. Financial advisors love to compare themselves to doctors, but I hope that doctors don't guess as much as financial advisors do. This isn't meant to be overcritical; it's just fact. You simply want your financial advisor to position you in the best possible manner so that you can do well in good markets and survive in bad markets. Anyone else that tells you they can do something different from this is lying. Come to think of it, this first quality should probably be "humility paired with knowledge." Your financial advisor should be able to give you confidence via his or her vulnerability. Several financial advisors try to gain your confidence by appearing all knowing. That's a bad idea, especially if a cat named Orlando just beat their returns.

▶ **Attentiveness.** No one likes to be ignored. I've accidentally neglected to return phone calls. I've accidentally neglected to return emails. Does this mean I'm terrible at customer service? To some, it may seem that way. The reality is that no matter the industry, customer service is really important, yet at times people make mistakes. When money is involved—all the money you have ever saved—things can get extra stressful when a phone call isn't returned. You'll know if your advisor is ducking you. You should meet with your advisor at least once per year, and the responsibility for setting up this meeting is shared.

▶ **Ability to teach.** Do you know what an American Depositary Receipt (ADR) is? No? That's okay; you wouldn't be in the minority. If you work with a good advisor for long enough, you will learn stuff like this and be better for it. I tend to eat at restaurants that make me a better home cook. Somehow, some way, I learn things about cooking by interacting with the waitstaff or kitchen staff. Have you been with a financial advisor for five years, yet you haven't learned anything? That's bad. Make sure you are a better investor for having known the advisor you're working with.

▶ **Risk radar.** Do you want to hear something crazy but true? I became a riskier investor, personally, when I stopped investing other people's money. Weird, right? I don't think so. My theory is that I never wanted my personal risk tolerance, derived from years of study and experience, to bleed over into my clients' risk tolerance. It'd be like trying to convince someone to like spicy food, despite the fact that it gives them ulcers.

If you don't want to take risks with your money, then don't. My least favorite thing about the investment industry is that if your advisor is wrong, then you are the one who suffers. You should dictate the direction of your investments by allowing the advisor to thoroughly measure your risk tolerance.

▶ **Reasonable fees.** Did you notice that I didn't say *fee only* or *commission only?* Why? Because, frankly, I've learned that it doesn't matter. The theory in the fee-based financial planning community (advisors that charge either a flat rate or a percentage of your assets invested) is that the only way to ensure objective advice is to limit compensation to the fee-based method. This is a fallacy. A commission salesperson isn't inherently biased. Would you rather have a commission-based financial advisor who knows what he or she is doing or a fee-based advisor who simply passed a test? Compensation structure is not a tell. You can't smoke out a crook by looking only at how someone is compensated. Some of the top Ponzi schemes of all time were perpetrated by fee-based advisors (Bernie Madoff). Just make sure your advisor has reasonable fees. And we'll leave it at that.

Here's the crazy thing about these five qualities: Everyone will measure them differently, just like wine. Some of my past clients may have thought I struggled at any one, if not all, of the qualities listed above. And because it's their perspective and their perspective alone, they'd be right. This is why advisor ratings—and wine ratings, for that matter—should be taken with a grain of salt. I've always thought advisor ratings were silly. I was once ranked as a top advisor at one of the firms I worked for. The rankings were based on production and nothing else. I was rated as excellent because I produced a lot of revenue for the firm, not because I was objectively good. Oddly enough, I've seen several advisors at the top of several companies leave the industry due to ethical and disciplinary issues. On top of that, many advisor ratings are linked to advertising buys.

This is why you should interview potential advisors and not just blindly go with the person a friend recommends. I love my friends, but I hate some of their wine recommendations. Do your best to try to evaluate these five qualities during your interview. My bottom line is this: You should be treated how you want to be treated by someone who knows what they're doing, all the while understanding your risk tolerance and charging you moderate fees.

But maybe the bigger point is this: You need to clean up your habits before you bother with an investment advisor, anyway.

FEES FOR A FINANCIAL ADVISOR

The financial planning industry has a practical yet insincere solution to the advisor selection quandary. The people in the industry have decided to turn the question into one of compensation. This path makes some sense, yet it offers close to zero solutions for those people without investable assets. In other words, if you don't have copious amounts of money to invest, then you will be passed over by the industry ethicists, the fee-based advisors, and fee-only advisors. This is where the confusion really begins.

There are primarily three ways in which financial advisors are compensated: commission-based, fee-based, and fee-only.

A commission-based advisor doesn't charge fees, but instead is compensated by investment and insurance companies upon selling their investments to consumers. And as crazy as this sounds, commission-based advisors have no industry-regulated responsibility to do what's in the client's best interest. This is called *fiduciary responsibility*, and commission-based advisors don't have it. Is a commission-based advisor predestined to give you biased financial advice based on potential commission rates? Arguably, but not always. Some experts argue that human nature prevents commission-based advisors from giving objective financial advice. I disagree.

A fee-based advisor charges a fee to manage investment assets and can still accept commissions from insurance and investment companies, whereas a fee-only advisor collects a fee for managing your money but doesn't accept any commission from third parties. The idea is to create an objective environment of fiduciary responsibility. However, the assertion that a fee-based or fee-only advisor is undeniably scrupulous is absurd. You do realize that speed-limit signs aren't suggestions, right? The main problem with this method is the imposition of "minimum assets" policies.

For a moment, let's say you have $8,000 to your name. Is that a lot of money? If you only have $8,000, then it's a tremendous amount of money. In fact, it's 100 percent of your money. Do you want it invested wisely? Yes. Do you want it invested in an unbiased way? Yes. Do you want someone to pick up the phone when you call to find someone to invest your money? Yes. The only person likely to pick up the phone is going to be a commission-based advisor.

This is a problem that the industry has created. The industry has basically said, "If you have $50,000 to invest, then we've got several ways in which the industry can objectively serve you." That doesn't work for me. Fee-based and fee-only advisors typically have minimum client requirements. I don't begrudge businesspeople's right to make business decisions on who they want or don't want as clients, but the scrutiny being placed on commission-based advisors for taking on smaller clients is unjust. This is all to say that picking your advisor based on how they're compensated is popular and convenient, but overrated.

No matter what type of advisor you choose, you owe it to yourself and your money to do a broker check. A broker check will allow you to see the regulatory history of your advisor. You'll be able to see complaints, judgments, and interesting patterns. Should you then make your judgment solely on what you find on the advisor's broker check? Nope. But I wouldn't consider hiring an advisor without first running a broker check. You can run a check on your advisor at BrokerCheck.FINRA.org.

RISK

Every person decides how much risk he or she is willing to deal with. What most people don't realize is that a person can't actually avoid risk. When people attempt to mitigate risk, they often expose themselves to different types of risk. This is especially true when it comes to financial planning.

Before we discuss some of the lesser-known financial risks, let's examine how someone arrives at his personal risk tolerance. Simply put, risk tolerance is a measure of how much risk a person is willing to accept in order to pursue investment returns. A low risk tolerance generally means a person isn't willing to have his or her savings or investments decrease in value due to market activity. On the other hand, a person with a high risk tolerance is willing to accept fluctuations in account values, even when account values dip into the negative. The biggest drivers of risk tolerance are personal experience and philosophy, knowledge level, and time horizon.

Nothing destroys a moderate risk tolerance quite like an investment portfolio getting hammered. Even if the investments were suitable, reasonable, and appropriate, investment loss can significantly affect a person's willingness to take future risk, even if and when the portfolio rises again. A negative experience can make people more introspective and conservative with their money.

I believe the number-one factor in determining risk tolerance is knowledge. People fear things they don't understand, as they should. If someone doesn't understand investments and the financial markets, frankly, they shouldn't proceed with investing anyway. The better solution would be to hire a trusted financial advisor, paired with a purposeful strategy to learn more about how the market works. If people don't know what they are doing, refuse to hire an advisor, and refuse to increase their financial education level, then they should have a low risk tolerance. It's self preservation. It's necessary.

The final factor in determining risk tolerance is time horizon. Risk tolerance and time horizon have a very important relationship. As a person gets closer to the need for saved money, time horizon shrinks, and risk tolerance will almost always decrease. For example, when you're 30 years out from retirement, you may have a higher risk tolerance than you would when you are 30 days out from retirement. Some people struggle to make wise retirement planning decisions because they don't account for time horizon. Instead, they make their investment decisions solely based on their long-developed risk tolerance. In my opinion, this is a mistake. My theory on risk is simple: Never take an ounce of market risk more than you need to in order to accomplish your goal. I believe both risk tolerance and time horizon are factors in making this decision.

And then there are the numbers. When doing some research for a retirement book, I learned that taking market risk makes a significant impact on retirement. Based on 5,000 simulations of a retirement scenario using historical market returns, a person with a portfolio of 50 percent bond, 30 percent cash, and 20 percent stock has an 89 percent chance of having money left over after taking annual withdrawals of 4 percent (of total portfolio value) for 30 years. A person who has a 100 percent cash portfolio (money market and savings), has a 19 percent chance of having any money left over, using the same withdrawal schedule. This makes the case that conservative investors often hurt themselves with conservative portfolio construction.

No one should invest against his or her risk tolerance. If you are a conservative investor, you are a conservative investor. There is no shame in that game. You shouldn't let anyone talk you out of being a conservative investor. The statistics above shouldn't even talk you out of being a conservative investor. Feel free to educate yourself on the markets and investing, but if that doesn't make you feel less conservative, then don't change unless you're willing to accept the risk.

CHAPTER 8

MAKING IT STICK

Have you ever made major diet and exercise changes on a whim, only to regress back into your old habits just weeks or months later? You have? Then that makes you normal. Change is hard. We struggle to permanently change our behavior for several reasons. If we don't see the desired and sometimes immediate results of our behavior shift, then we are likely to seek familiar ground, no matter how unstable that familiar ground can be.

When you set up your Commissioner pool and begin paying yourself a salary, you may face setbacks of varying degrees. Surviving months will come, tires will flatten, and your higher-earning months may seem few and far between. Adversity has happened in the past, and it will continue to happen in the future. However, this time you have a system and a strategy. So when adversity comes, don't abandon ship. You must trust the process. The process will allow you to develop new financial skills to match the technical skills you use every day in your career. And trust me when I tell you that this *is* a process. It isn't a small financial diet or the money equivalent to six-minute abs. The process of stabilizing your financial life takes time and has many moving pieces.

Your technical skills create revenue. That revenue flows into your pool. That pool pays your salary. Your salary was determined by your budget. Your salary will handle your monthly bills and help you systematically pay down debt. Your salary will help you build wealth. That's how your new machine works. If any one part of this process breaks down, you are in trouble. To make sure this doesn't happen, you will need a maintenance plan.

While focusing on the positive is healthy, trying to identify what could go wrong is a vital part of the growth process. As you think through your sales process, including the pool and salary payment, you need to identify any potential weak points that could break your machine. Even the best processes in the world can break down if there are flaws in some of the independent parts.

Not to cast a pessimistic light on the situation, but you need to be on the lookout for setbacks. To make sure these setbacks don't turn into convenient excuses, you'll need to have a deep understanding of the main pressure points of your income process. Specifically, watch out for four common setbacks.

ERODING PROFESSIONAL SKILLS

When you decided to fix your personal financial life, you decided to give your career a boost. Your career and your personal finances have a symbiotic relationship. They need each other to exist at all. If you've struggled financially in the past, it may have been the result of relying on your professional successes to fuel your personal finances. And while focusing on work certainly improved your professional competency, it probably didn't solve any financial problem. A lack of resourcefulness is typically the cause of financial ills, not a lack of resources, even when those resources are produced by career excellence.

Conversely, if you focus on your personal finances, you can take the pressure off of your career. Creating and maintaining a healthy financial lifestyle will allow you to focus on career progression and contentment, not just producing revenue. Here's what you *can't* do: waste the opportunity to move your career forward. Gaining and maintaining control of your finances is freeing, but you can't waste this free feeling by letting your work-life slip. It can happen, especially if you start viewing money differently. When more money stops being the solution, your newfound perspective can be dangerous for your career.

You will be forced to make a very simple decision: Are you going use your new money perspective to slow down at work, or are you going to harness your new perspective to take calculated career risks and improve your professional skill set? Think of it this way: If you ate healthy and ran every morning in an effort to lose weight, would you stop eating healthy and running every morning once you lost the weight? Use the momentum in your financial life to create momentum at work. Don't just sit back and waste the results you've worked so hard to accomplish.

DWINDLING POOL

In the early days of paying yourself a Commissioner's salary, your Commissioner pool may dwindle. And despite all the financial progress you've made, both with your skills and your awareness, a low pool will equal high stress. Don't abandon ship. It will take you up to six months to create reliable stability.

If the stress continues to increase and you find yourself in surviving month after surviving month, taking the pressure off
your pool with an additional income stream might be the way
to go.

INCREASED SALARY NEED

Normally, we are wholly responsible for our financial
obligations. This was true before you started reading
The Commissioner, and this will be true after you've completed
The Commissioner. But now you understand how much pressure you put on your income and budget when you increase
your monthly expenses. You will now have a much more measured approach to consumer purchases, both big and small.

However, sometimes you truly can't control the expenses that
arrive in your life, and you certainly can't control the timing.
For instance, if your car needs major repairs before your emergency fund is built up, then you may be forced to increase your
salary need either temporarily or permanently to pay for the
repairs. If it's at all humanly possible, it would make more
sense to try to decrease spending in other categories, prior to
increasing your income—thus keeping your income need static.

Thinking back, I had a major involuntary increase in expenses
when my health-insurance premium nearly doubled. I bridged
the gap by reducing spending in some other key discretionary
spending categories and increasing my Commissioner salary.

Inflation is a real economic concept that affects most people.
It will probably affect you, too. Many salaried people receive
an annual cost-of-living adjustment (COLA)—or a raise, as

you might call it—to specifically battle the money-zapping power of inflation. When increasing prices begin to hit your Commissioner plan, be judicious when deciding to give yourself a raise.

BOREDOM AND COMPLACENCY

If you've never had true financial stability in your life, you'll find that financial stability can create some strange behaviors and reactions. Stability doesn't always inspire further financial greatness. Sometimes it creates complacency.

For instance, if you need to have $15,000 in your emergency fund, yet you've never been able to achieve this in the past, finally reaching your goal may result in a giant exhale, and not the springboard to financial wellness you need. Even if you left your financial past behind by paying off debt, and you've stabilized your present with a proper emergency fund, there is still the future. The future is as vast as it is unpredictable. Financial wellness is achieved when the past is rectified, the present is stabilized, and the future is secured. Every time you feel yourself letting up on the gas, revisit the wealth chapter of this book. You may feel as though you have plenty of money for your financial goals, but it's your use of time that will really determine your success.

Complacency can also lead to you lying to yourself. Telling yourself financial lies is bad news. I've had hundreds, if not thousands, of people lie to me about their financial lives. I don't really care whether they're lying, because I usually have the numbers in front of me, and the numbers rarely lie. I'm usually more concerned that people believe their own lies. When someone starts lying to me, I think, "I wonder if they believe this lie." If they do believe the lies they're spewing, they're in trouble. Believing your own lies is always a recipe for a financial disaster.

Here are the five biggest lies variable income-earners tell themselves on a regular basis. Have you told yourself any of these?

▶ **I've got plenty of time to save for retirement.** No you don't. Two factors are important in any accumulation plan: money and time. You need both. You need to invest money for the future. And you need time to do what time does. Time is the most important element of retirement savings, and forgoing it for any reason is a mistake.

▶ **I spend the same amount of money on my credit card as I would if I were to use just my debit card for monthly spending.** You need to understand that your use of credit can be especially dangerous when you live on a variable income. While you might think you're using credit as a tool to bridge the gap during challenging times, you may be forming really bad habits. For instance, consistent credit card use, even when paid off at the end of each month, can lead to more aggressive spending.

I've never heard a debit card user say, "I spend between $1,500 and $3,500 per month on my debit card." Do you know who says that sort of thing? People who use their credit card for everything and then pay it off at the end of the month. While refusing to carry over a balance is a good practice, it also creates a blank-check mentality that induces freer spending. You don't have to believe me—just put down your credit card for one month and do all your spending on your debit card. You will spend less. And I don't care about the reward points you earn by using your credit card.

▶ **I have plenty of life insurance.** You probably don't. I've never quite understood people's general aversion to life insurance. We're all going to die. You don't seal your fate if you buy life insurance. You actually seal your fate if you *don't* buy life insurance. Why would you want your significant other and/or children to suffer financially at your eventual demise? When you die, your income dies. And if your family depends on your income, then you are putting them in a terrible position. Skip a few trips to a casual dining restaurant and buy the right amount of life insurance. Most people need about 10 times their annual income in life insurance.

▶ **I'm very aware of my finances. I check my bank balances daily.** Do you know what online banking has done to financial awareness in this country? It has killed it. And not in a good way. Online banking has become a financial crutch for the apathetic. Do you think people in the 1980s looked at their check registers every single day? No, they didn't. Did they save more of their disposable income? Yes. Did they have less consumer debt? Yes. Online banking is a convenience tool, not a financial tool. If you were financially aware, you wouldn't need to look so often.

▶ **I don't need financial goals. They're stupid and point-less.** You have sales and income goals, right? So don't stop there. You need goals for your personal finances, too. I don't understand why salespeople fight personal finance goals, but they often do. Take the next step and establish some personal finance goals.

Don't feel anxiety over writing goals. You aren't sign-ing up to walk on hot coals; you're simply letting a piece of paper know what's going on inside of your brain. The strangest thing about writing down finan-cial goals is it actually makes your financial life easier, not harder. Sure, some goals will cause you to increase your effort, but most of the time goals just allow you to better focus whatever effort you are currently giv-ing. Start with 30-day financial goals. What would you like to accomplish financially in the next 30 days? How much money will that require? How would accomplishing this goal affect your life?

You can lie to me. You can lie to your friends. You can lie to your spouse. You can lie to your boss. You can lie to your dog. You can lie to your financial planner. You can lie to your hair-stylist. You can lie to your therapist. You can lie to the IRS. You can lie to everyone at your high school reunion. Just don't lie to yourself.

THE COMMISSIONER RULES

I hate to slap rules on you so late in the book, but there are Commissioner rules that you must consider. Do not, I repeat, *do not* break the rules. I can think of a million reasons why you might want to break the rules, convenience being 950,000 of them, but don't do it. The Commissioner rules are vital to your long-term success, not just your short-term survival.

Live these rules.

- ▶ You must determine your monthly need.

- ▶ All revenue must pass through the pool, including bonuses paid by your employer.

- ▶ Your pool is not your emergency fund.

- ▶ A raise or bonus must meet the pool requirements.

- ▶ You must contribute to your employer-sponsored retirement plan, at least to the match, while working on debt reduction, filling the pool, and/or funding your emergency fund. If your employer doesn't offer a retirement plan, open an IRA or a Roth IRA on your own.

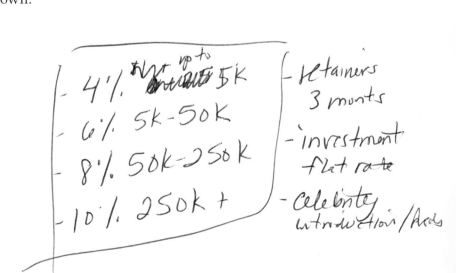

YOUR INCOME IS NO LONGER ARBITRARY

Although this book is near its end, your work is not. You must continue to focus on creating the financial life you desire by focusing on creating stability. Your diligence and measured patience will pay off. Your ability to generate wealth—and, more importantly, avoid unnecessary financial obligations— will allow you to live a stress-free financial life.

There are plenty of additional resources for you at PeteThePlanner.com/Commissioner. And I'm just a tweet away at @PeteThePlanner. Best of luck, and may you never go hungry. You are the Commissioner.

INDEX

F

family and friends, personal loans from, 30–31
federal (subsidized) student loans, 20
fee-based financial advisor, 134–137
fee-only financial advisors, 135–137
fiduciary responsibility, 136
finance resources, 151
financial advisors
  attentiveness, 133
  broker checks, 137
  commission-based, 136–137
  fee-based, 134–137
  fee-only, 135–137
  fees, 135–137
  hiring, 130–140
  knowledge level, 132
  qualities of, 134
  ratings, 135
  risk assessment, 133–134
  risk tolerance assessment, 137–140
  selecting, 130–131
financial rules, 150
financial stress
  academic-performance issues by children of parents dealing with, 4
  AP-AOL poll on, 4
  forcing income to match expenses, 9–10
  goals, 12
  health issues caused by, 4
  honest assessment of, 11
  ignoring, 4
  loss of productivity, presenteeism, and poor-on-the-job decision making, 4
  mismanaging, 10
  stress test, 10–11

financial-independence, 122–123
fixed expenses, 3
food budgets, 54–56
frequency of pay, 2
funds
  Exchange Traded Funds (ETFs), 111–112, 117
  index, 111–112
  mutual, 110–111, 117
  target-date, 112–114

G

gift budgets, 59–60
glide path, 112
goals
  anxiety toward, 149
  attitude of boredom and complacency toward, 149
  financial stress, 12
Good Debt/Bad Debt ratings
  bank credit cards, 22–23
  basic description of, 17–18
  car loans, 25
  collection debt, 32
  home loans, 25–26
  judgments, 33
  lines of credit, 28
  medical debt, 26–27
  payday loans, 29
  personal loans (from family and friends), 31
  personal loans (from financial institution), 30
  store credit cards, 24
  student loans, 21
  tax debt, 31
greed, 102

O

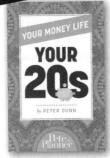
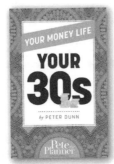